SHEPHERDS OF THE FAITH

SHEPHERDS OF THE FAITH

1843-1993

A Brief History of the Bishops of the Catholic Diocese of Pittsburgh

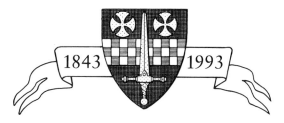

by
Monsignor Francis A. Glenn

edited by
R. Stephen Almagno, O.F.M.,
and
Marylynne Pitz

Catholic Diocese of Pittsburgh

CONTENTS

CONTENTS

Foreword

History is the telling of the story of a people. The shared experiences of a people hold them together and help identify them. There are different ways of telling our story and many voices that echo aspects of the rich tales of our individual and collective pilgrimage as God's people over this past century and a half. Institutions and public figures act as milestones along the way of our journey, but we are all aware that the joyful, sorrowful and glorious mysteries in the lives of all our people are the fiber out of which the fabric of this Church is woven.

For the past 150 years, the story of the Church at Pittsburgh has involved her bishops in a particular way, beginning with Bishop Michael J. O'Connor who was appointed in 1843 to head this local Church. This present volume highlights the eleven bishops who were called and privileged to serve as chief shepherds of this faith family that is so rich in its commitment to the Lord, its love of God and its works of goodness to its neighbors.

As we trace in broad strokes the history of this Church, we are also reminded that Christ identified himself with all of his followers. To the disciples, as he sent them to preach in his name, he said: "Whoever listens to you listens to me and whoever rejects you rejects me" (Lk. 10.16). To those who did deeds of charity for his little ones he proclaimed: "Just as you did it to one of the least of these who are members of my family, you did it to me" (Matt. 25.40). At the Last Supper our Lord spoke of the intense unity that makes him one with those who are united by faith and love to him. "I am the vine, you are the branches" (Jn. 15.5). The vine and the branches are one living reality. So it is also with Christ and his Church, Christ and those who love him. Such is the unity and identity with Christ which the entire Church of Pittsburgh has sought to maintain and seeks now to continue living.

As we read in these pages of the pilgrimage of God's people in southwestern Pennsylvania highlighted in the activities of their shepherds, we thank God for the call that has challenged us to be a community that praises God, for the love shown us in Jesus Christ and for the grace to build up this community in faith, in love, and in the Spirit.

† Donald W. Wuerl
Bishop of Pittsburgh

August, 1993

Preface

The evil that men do lives after them;
The good is oft interred with their bones.
Shakespeare, *Julius Caesar* 3.2

Substituting "problems men endured" for "evil that men do," Mark Antony's reflection on the life of Julius Ceasar summarizes the disparity between the achievements of the bishops of Pittsburgh and the difficulties experienced in the governance of the Diocese. Great accomplishments become mere statistics, while controversies are recorded for posterity.

Bishop Michael O'Connor's proficiency in organizing the Diocese of Pittsburgh is overshadowed by vexations of bigots like Mayor Joe Barker, and acrimonious attacks by newspapers.

In the episcopates of Bishop Michael Domenec and Bishop John Tuigg, wonderful successes in meeting the needs of their adherents were obscured by civil litigations and internal disputes which interfered with their dedicated efforts.

The length of a chapter in this story is not indicative of its importance in the history of the Diocese of Pittsburgh. Most bishops experienced very active, progressive years of service that witnessed great development of the Diocese without extraneous disturbances to the quiet expansion in members and services.

Monsignor Andrew A. Lambing is recognized as the greatest historian of the Catholic Church in western Pennsylvania in the nineteenth century. His collections of historical data and his publications of histories pertaining to the Diocese of Pittsburgh are invaluable resources of historical knowledge.

For many years, Father John Canova, Pastor of St. Alphonsus

Church, Murrinsville, collected and chronicled Msgr. Lambing's trove of manuscripts. He established the Historical Archives of the Diocese of Pittsburgh, now maintained by Father Edward McSweeney. These Historical Archives are in the Diocesan Archives and Records Center, under the supervision of Mr. Kenneth White.

A diocese is established when a bishop is assigned to administer the affairs of the church in a specific territory. A natural outline of the history of a diocese is determined by the terms of the individual bishops, and each epoch of a diocese is marked and remembered in reference to the bishop of that time.

Editorial limitations preclude including the accomplishments of the religious orders of women and men; the scope of Catholic education on all levels; and the successes of social and health services of the Diocese. The variety of ethnic traditions and other facets of activities of the Church have necessarily been deleted in this story of the bishops of the Pittsburgh Diocese.

Msgr. Francis A. Glenn gratefully acknowledges the assistance of: R. Stephen Almagno, O.F.M., and Marylynne Pitz (editors), Fr. Ronald Lengwin (Diocese of Pittsburgh, Department of Public Affairs), Mr. Kenneth White and Fr. Edward McSweeney (Diocese of Pittsburgh, Diocesan Archives and Records Center), Bishop John B. McDowell, Kerry Crawford, Paul Dvorchak, John F. Farmerie, Msgr. Joseph G. Findlan, Sr. Anna Mary Gibson, R.S.M., Fr. W. Peter Horton, Jerry Jansen, Mary K. Johnsen, Anthony P. Joseph, Jr., Fr. Joseph A. Kopecky, Fr. David Kriss, Joseph Makarewicz, Rebecca Mertz, Sr. Cecilia Murphy, R.S.M., Blanche McGuire, Fr. Steven M. Palsa, Fr. Joseph C. Scheib, Fr. Henry Szarnicki, Fr. Richard Ward and Sr. Sally Witt, C.S.J. (Members of the Catholic Historical Society of Western Pennsylvania), Dorothy Fafata and Ruth Fafata (typing and computer), and the Hunkele Foundation.

Introduction

Brownsville, Pennsylvania
July 25, 1835

Sacred Congregation for the
Propagation of the Faith:

From the visitation of the diocese which I am making for the fifth
time, it appears to me clearly to the advantage of the Church's work
to have the Diocese of Philadelphia divided and to erect a new
episcopal see in Pittsburgh. I am convinced that it would be to the
advantage of the spiritual life, if a bishop be placed over the western
part of Pennsylvania.

The City of Pittsburgh is quite large, it is strong in resources and
good men and has a population of 20,000. It has two churches, one
of which is new and was dedicated under the invocation of St. Paul.
In size and beauty it easily surpasses any other church in Pennsylvania.
There are 6,000 Catholics in the city, including the immediate
neighborhood and many thousands in the whole district.

(Signed) † Francis Patrick Kenrick
Administrator and Bishop of Philadelphia[1]

Bishop Kenrick, writing in 1835, was not the first to recommend establishing a diocese in Pittsburgh. Bp. Flaget, Father Demetrius A. Gallitzin, and the Provincial Councils of Baltimore had also expressed the need for a diocese in western Pennsylvania.

In 1792, the Sulpician Fr. Benedict J. Flaget — who, while en route to Vincennes, Indiana, had to wait in Pittsburgh for the Ohio River to rise to a navigable level — ministered to the needs of Catholics in the area. In 1823, when he was bishop of Bardstown, Kentucky, Flaget visited Pittsburgh, recognized the need for a diocesan bishop, and began to press for the establishment of a diocese.[2]

Also in 1823, Fr. Demetrius A. Gallitzin, pastor at Loretto and vicar-general for western Pennsylvania, suggested to Ambrose Marechal, archbishop of Baltimore, that a diocese be established in western Pennsylvania. But Gallitzin preferred that Loretto be the site.

In the early decades of the nineteenth century, the population of the Commonwealth of Pennsylvania continued to increase. The Diocese of Philadelphia, which was composed of Pennsylvania, Delaware and part of New Jersey, also expanded. However, 20 years would pass before the Diocese of Philadelphia would be divided. On June 6, 1830, Francis P. Kenrick was appointed coadjutor to the bishop of Philadelphia. The aged and infirm Henry Conwell, who served as diocesan bishop of Philadelphia from 1820–1824, retained the title, but Kenrick, a renowned theologian and apologist, assumed full charge of the Diocese of Philadelphia.

Bp. Kenrick's *Diary and Visitation Record* is the most authentic and reliable source of information about the growth of the church and the foundation of the first parishes in western Pennsylvania. In it, Kenrick — who between 1830 and 1843 made twelve visits to the area — described his activities with persons and parishes, and his resolution of controversies.[3]

From personal experience, Kenrick knew how to avoid some of the problems that were common in the early years of the nineteenth century. Having been successful in a stand-off with the trustees of the Philadelphia Cathedral which marred his arrival in that city in 1830, he insisted that all church properties be recorded in the name of the bishop, in trust for the congregation.

Traveling from settlement to settlement by wagon, horseback, or on foot, presented a variety of hardships. Bishop Kenrick's entry in his *Diary and Visitation Record* for May 26, 1834, is an example of one day in the life of a missionary bishop:

> We took the stage on the way to the town of Centreville. We passed the night making this journey and at seven o'clock in the morning we reached the town of Meadville. No Catholic was known to us living in this town, and, although we offered to pay, no one would take us in a heavy wagon to the Catholics who live sixteen miles distant near Cussawago Creek. Therefore, we started out on foot hoping to find perchance some Catholic on the way. When we had walked two miles we met Edward Tinney and a Mr. Sweeney, who brought horses for us to ride. We remained in the house of Miles Tinney who had been living here thirty four years. The next day which was the feast of Corpus Christi, we celebrated mass in a church lately built of the trunks of trees. The church still wants windows and has no door. Three persons received the Sacrament of holy Chrism; they had gotten notice of the visitation only two days before. Thirty-five received Holy Communion; seventeen infants were baptized.[4]

The need of a diocese in western Pennsylvania became an almost constant petition to the Vatican. In 1836, documents for the establishment of a diocese in Pittsburgh were prepared in Rome, but never executed. These documents named Kenrick as diocesan Bishop of Pittsburgh, and Fr. John Hughes as Bishop of Philadelphia. In 1837, the Third Provincial Council of Baltimore renewed the proposal, but it was rejected.

On May 14, 1843, at the Fifth Provincial Council of Baltimore, the proposal was accepted and the recommendation forwarded to Rome. On August 8, 1843, the document establishing the *Diocese of Western Pennsylvania* was signed by Pope Gregory XVI. The bishops of Philadelphia and Pittsburgh determined that the counties in the western part of the state would form the new diocese.[5]

One

Catholicism in the United States

Go therefore and make disciples of all nations. . . .
Matthew 28.19

A strong building requires a firm foundation. The story of the Catholic Church in western Pennsylvania could begin with the events and experiences of Bishop Francis Kenrick and his proposals for establishing a diocese in the city of Pittsburgh.

The foundation for the spread of the Catholic faith in the western hemisphere was laid by Christopher Columbus, and the French and Spanish explorers who followed played a part in the planting of the faith and its extension throughout the United States.

In his classic book, *Admiral of the Ocean Sea: A Life of Christopher Columbus*, Samuel Eliot Morison describes the initial voyage of Christopher Columbus. He relates how on the morning of October 12, 1492, as Columbus landed on Watling Island in the Bahamas, he knelt down, implanted the Cross of Christ, and gave thanks to God for the success of his endeavors.[1]

Christopher Columbus was searching for a short way to the Orient. For the Kingdom of Spain, he was seeking the spices and treasures of the East, but he was also motivated to be a missionary and to evangelize non-Christians with the knowledge and teaching of Jesus Christ. Before launching his ships, Columbus consecrated his voyage to God's protection. As soon as he reached land, he dedicated it to San Salvador — Holy Savior.

Catholicism came early and played an important role in the origin of America. Immediately after Columbus's first voyage, the Catholic faith was established in the New World. On June 25, 1493, Alexander VI, by his letter *Pius Fidelium*, named Father Bernard Buil (Boyle) to be vicar-apostolic of the newly discovered lands. The vicar-apostolic accompanied Columbus on his second voyage in September, 1493.

The mistreatment of the natives in the western hemisphere by some of the European explorers and colonists had clouded the main purposes and achievements of the courageous navigators who sailed uncharted seas in the sixteenth century. Enslavement of the natives was always resisted by priests who accompanied the explorations. In 1510, Fr. Antonio Montesnio, O.P., protested the mistreatment of Native Americans. In 1512, King Ferdinand of Spain, in a primary enactment of a civil rights law, decreed the *Law of Burgos* which was intended to safeguard the natives. Unfortunately, the enforcement of these laws was entrusted to persons who were exploiting the natives, so the situation did not necessarily improve.

Opposition to mistreatment of the natives continued. In 1515, Fr. Bartolomeo de Las Casas, O.P., began his persistent demands for the abolition of all slavery. Church and State attempted to respond to his denunciations. Paul III, in 1537, condemned the enslavement of Indians, and in 1565 Emperor Charles V incorporated reform proposals in his *New Laws* regarding these peoples. The courageous protests of the missionaries, while not always successful, did preserve many Native Americans from more grievous treatment by their conquerors.[2]

The conquest of territory and the spread of the faith were concurrent motivations for the prime explorers in the New World. In 1565, King Philip II of Spain commissioned Don Pedro Menendez de Aviles to conquer and convert Florida. On September 8, 1565, Menendez sighted Cape Canaveral. And when Menendez landed, he founded the city of St. Augustine, the first permanent settlement on this continent. In his report to King Philip, on September 11, Menendez dedicated the success of his voyage "To the great service of God Our Lord, for the increase of our Holy Catholic Faith, and for the service of your Majesty."[3]

The early history of European explorations in the New World was almost entirely Catholic. Hundreds of years before the United States officially became an independent nation, explorers from France, Spain, and other Catholic countries crisscrossed North America in trips of discovery and adventure. Catholic chaplains accompanied these explorers, and it was customary for these priests to offer Mass whenever possible.

Thirty-four years after Columbus's first voyage, Spanish colonists attempted a settlement on the Chesapeake, which they called the *Bay of the Mother of God*. This was in 1526, almost a century before the English establishment of Jamestown, Virginia.[4]

Jacques Cartier, the French explorer, in 1534, took possession of the St. Lawrence River Valley, and of North America in general, in the name of the French sovereign. Almost a century elapsed before the French settled in that region. When they did come they were accompanied by priests who extended their mission into what is now Maine.

In 1604, Fr. Nicholas Aubry established a mission on Docket Island at the St. Croix River, and in 1609, two Jesuits, Fr. Peter Biard and Fr. Enemond Masse, built a chapel on Neutral Island. The site was an unsuitable location, and after three years they relocated to Mt. Desert Island and established the mission of St. Sauveur. The Puritan settlers in New England resented the proximity of the Catholic mission. In 1613, a Puritan army from Virginia under the command of English Captain Samuel Argall destroyed the mission and deported the priests to France.[5]

The destruction of the mission did not stop the Jesuits' work. In 1646, a delegation of Native American tribal chiefs from the banks of the Kennebec River journeyed to the Jesuit House at Sillery, in Canada, where they asked that a priest be sent to live with them. Jesuit Fr. Gabriel Druillettes was sent in response to the chiefs' request. He and his successor, Fr. Sebastian Rale, are noted for their accomplishments among the Abenaki tribe. The lives and works of these priests are exemplary models and lasting inspirations.[6]

There was a fundamental difference between the French explorers and their English counterparts, as the French sought not only to expand territory, but also to convert the natives to Christianity. For the French, a chaplain was an indispensable partner in every expedition. Theoretically, the English proclaimed the same ideals, but they did not follow through in performance.

Generally, the French treated the native people well. They mingled with them, and sometimes even intermarried. When the French established a new settlement they usually lived in peace with the tribes of the neighborhood. This was in marked contrast to the English practice of driving tribes from their villages and confiscating their land.

Fr. Sebastian Rale was murdered in 1724 by English soldiers under the command of Capts. Harmon and Moulton when they destroyed his mission along the Kennebec River. Fr. Rale's dictionary of the Abenaki language was saved and taken to Boston.

Not long after this pillage, Governor Thomas Dudley of Massachusetts tried to persuade the Abenaki people to renounce the Catholic faith. He offered to rebuild their chapel if they would choose a Protestant minister instead of a Catholic "black gown." When the Abenaki chief heard this singular offer, he arose with great dignity and said:

> You were here first, and saw me a long time before the French governors, but neither you nor your ministers spoke to me of prayer or the Great Spirit. You saw my furs, my beaver and moose skins, and of these only did you think then. But when the French black gown came, though I was loaded with furs, he disdained to look at them. He spoke to me of the Great Spirit, of heaven and hell, of the prayer which is the only way to reach heaven. I heard him, and I was delighted with his words. At last the prayer pleased me. I asked to be instructed, and finally baptized. Thus have the French acted. Had you spoken to me of this prayer as soon as we met, I should now be so unhappy as to pray like you, for I could not have told whether your prayers were good or bad. Now I hold to the prayer of the French — I agree to it. I shall be faithful to it, even until the earth is destroyed. I will go to my French fathers.[7]

The earliest French settlements were along the St. Lawrence River. The colonists were deeply Catholic and full of missionary zeal. Fearless Catholic trappers and adventurers sailed down the natural waterway of the St. Lawrence to the Great Lakes. They established a network of settlements and trading posts from Canada down the Mississippi to New Orleans.

In the seventeenth century, most explorations covered the Great Lakes and down the Mississippi River. In 1669–1670, Rene Robert Cavelier de La Salle altered this course and discovered the *Belle Riviere* — the Ohio River. When de La Salle departed Montreal he was accompanied by two Sulpicians, Frs. DeCasson and DeGalinee. During the course of the journey, the priests were convinced, apparently by Louis Joliet, that there was a greater need for them among the Potowami Indians in the northwest, and they left de La Salle's expedition for this more urgent field of mission. There is no record of the chaplains accompanying de La Salle through western Pennsylvania.[8]

Although some historians have disputed the claim that de La Salle discovered the Ohio River, there is much evidence that he did. A manuscript map of the Allegheny and Ohio Rivers, drawn in 1673 bears the legend: "The Ohio River, so called by the Iroquois on account of its beauty, which Sieur de La Salle descended." The renowned historian Francis Parkman supported this claim. Two maps by Louis Joliet, made in 1674, bear similar notations. George Washington, in his 1754 report to Governor Dinwiddie, refers to de La Salle as the discoverer of the Ohio River.[9]

Western Pennsylvania became a focus of contention. The French had a compelling reason to restrict access to the Ohio River Valley. The English also desired the territory. The Appalachian Mountains formed a natural barrier through the Commonwealth of Pennsylvania and most of the residents lived on the east side of that range. The French realized that if they could control the Ohio and Mississippi Rivers they could constrain the English in the eastern side of the Appalachians.

In the early years of the eighteenth century, the western section of Pennsylvania was claimed by the French, the English, and by the family of William Penn. The French based their claim on their explorations. The Penn family asserted their right by grants from the English royalty. The English demanded possession because the Treaty of Utrecht of 1713 assigned them all of the territory inhabited by the Iroquois people.[10]

In Europe, the war between the French and English came to an end in 1697. But in America, both countries prepared to strengthen their claims to the western region of Pennsylvania. To regularly reinforce their claim and to keep in contact with the Native American tribes, the French sent expeditions of soldiers and explorers into the district every ten years.

In 1729, a civil engineer named M. De Lery led an expedition and made a careful survey of the Ohio River valley. The chaplain's name, however, was not recorded.

In 1739, an expedition supervised by Baron Charles LeMoyne Longueil had three chaplains. Fr. Vernet, a Franciscan, was chaplain to the Canadian soldiers. Fr. de La Bretonniere, a Jesuit, and Fr. W. du Perret, a Sulpician, were chaplains to the 319 Native Americans taking part in the expedition. It is noteworthy that two chaplains were assigned to meet the needs of the native peoples, too often considered uneducated savages. This assignment emphasizes their high status in the eyes of the French. Missionaries had already been working to convert the natives for a century before this expedition.

The Abenakis of Maine had petitioned for a resident priest in 1646, and there are records of missionaries working among the Senecas in 1672. Some of the tribes on Longueil's expedition could have had a Catholic background for more than a hundred years. The diary of one of the engineers on this expedition, Joseph Gaspard Chautegros de Lery, son of the leader of the 1729 survey, records that the priests said Mass often.[11]

The most celebrated of these expeditions was led by Captain Pierre Joseph Celeron de Blainville in 1749. The chaplain was Jesuit Fr. Joseph Pierre de Bonnecamps, a mathematician. Celeron and Fr. Bonnecamps both wrote journals of this expedition. Fr. Bonnecamps also drew a map of the territory marking longitude and latitude of the places where they stopped. At various places along the river banks, they planted heavy lead plates to maintain the French claim of ownership. Fr. Bonnecamps recorded dates and places where they encamped as well. On Wednesday, July 30, they were at Warren, Pennsylvania. On that day he noted the first specific record of a definite place where Mass was offered in western Pennsylvania. On Thursday, August 7, they camped at what is now Tarentum. On August 8, they were at McKees Rocks, and from August 9 to August 12, they remained at Logstown, a native village, near the present Byersdale, between Ambridge and Baden.[12]

The English government was also anxious to support its claim to the western Pennsylvania territory. On October 31, 1753, Virginia Governor Robert Dinwiddie sent Major George Washington to the French garrison at Fort LeBouef. Washington complained that the French were encroaching on English territory. The French were unimpressed by this admonition, and Major Washington was rebuffed. In his report to Dinwiddie, Washington described Fort LeBouef and noted that it contained a chapel dedicated to Saint Peter. The fort was located in what is now Waterford, Pennsylvania.

Returning from this unsuccessful journey, Washington recommended erecting a fort at the junction of the Allegheny and Monongahela Rivers, named "The Forks" by some Native American groups. In 1754, Dinwiddie ordered the construction of Fort Prince George at the Forks, and sent a small contingent to begin work.

Washington's trip to Fort LeBouef awakened the French to the designs of the English. The French accelerated their military excursions into the Ohio Valley. On April 16, 1754, a French expedition of more than 600 men, led by Captain P. Claude de Contrecouer, expelled the small English garrison stationed at the Forks. They destroyed the incomplete Fort Prince George, and began to erect Fort Duquesne at the site.

The chaplain of Contrecouer's expedition was Franciscan Fr. Denys Baron. On April 17, 1754, Fr. Baron offered the first Mass within the present city of Pittsburgh. Fr. Baron's record of baptisms and burials at Fort Duquesne, 1754–1756, indicates that within Fort Duquesne was a chapel dedicated to *The Assumption of the Blessed Virgin at the Beautiful River*.

The *Register of Fort Duquesne*, kept in the Archives of the city of Montreal, Canada, shows that Fr. Baron ministered to the soldiers in the fort and the people who lived nearby. His records show that he cared for the people of Native American, Irish, and English heritage.[13]

Even before the fall of Fort Prince George, Major George Washington was arranging to assist Capt. William Trent at that fort. After he learned that the fort had been destroyed, Washington remained determined to continue his advance and to recapture it.

The French garrison, suspecting English retaliation, sent a small reconnaissance group, under the command of Ensign Joseph Coulon de Jumonville, to try to determine the size and route of an English force. When Jumonville's group arrived at the Chestnut Ridge of the Appalachian Mountains, they were not far from Washington's force, which was camped at Great Meadows.

Aware of the presence of the French in the vicinity, Washington surprised Jumonville's detachment on the morning of May 28. Twelve men, including Jumonville, were killed. Two soldiers escaped, and the two remaining were taken prisoners. This small skirmish was the formal

Fort Duquesne. 81

In the year one thousand seven hundred and fifty-six, on the fifth of December, died at Fort Duquesne, under the title of the Assumption of the Blessed Virgin at the Beautiful River, (a man) named Thomas Jiroux, aged twenty-one years, or thereabout, after having received the holy sacraments of Penance, and Extreme Unction. His remains were interred in the smallpox[47] cemetery, and that with the customary ceremonies, by us, Recollect priest, the undersigned chaplain of the King, at the abovementioned Fort Duquesne. In testimony whereof we have signed :

Interment of Thomas Jiroux, of the parish of St. Thomas.

Fr. DENYS BARON, P. R.,
Chaplain.

In the year one thousand seven hundred and fifty-six, on the seventeenth of December, was baptized with the customary ceremonies of our Holy Mother the Roman Catholic Church, John Baptist Christiguay,[48] Great Chief (of the) Iroquois, aged ninety-five years, or thereabout, who being dangerously sick, earnestly desired Holy Baptism, which was administered the same day as above, by us, Recollect priest, the undersigned chaplain of the King at Fort Duquesne. The god-father was the Sieur Chavaudray, interpreter of the Iroquois, who signed with us.

Baptism of the aged Christiguay, Great Chief of the Iroquois,

JH. CHAVAUDRAYE.
Fr. DENYS BARON, P. R.,
Chaplain.[49]

In the year one thousand seven hundred and fifty-six, on the twenty-fifth of December, was baptized conditionally, by us, Recollect priest, the undersigned chaplain of the King at Fort Duquesne, under the title of the Assumption of the Blessed Virgin at the Beautiful River, Louis, of English parentage, aged eighteen months, or thereabout, the name of whose father and mother was unknown, whose father is a prisoner among the Loup (Mohegan) Indians, and who being dangerously sick, I, Recollect priest, the undersigned chaplain of the King at the abovementioned fort, certify to have administered to him the sacrament of Baptism, and that with the customary ceremonies of our

Baptism of Louis, of English parentage, the name of whose father and mother is unknown.

11

This page from the *Register of Fort Duquesne, 1754–56,* translated from French, records the baptism of an Iroquois chief and other occurences.

beginning of the French and Indian War.[15]

After conquering Jumonville, Washington retreated to the Great Meadows and hastily built a small palisade fort which he named Fort Necessity. Soon afterward, reinforced with a contingent of 400 additional men, Washington received word of a large French force advancing against him. This army was under the command of Coulon de Villiers, a half-brother of Jumonville, who had demanded this leadership so that he could avenge his brother's death.

The chaplain to this army was Franciscan Fr. Gabriel Anheuser. When they had encamped near McKeesport, de Villiers recorded in his diary: "Mass was said in camp, after which we marched."[16]

Washington's advance was so arduous, and the approaching enemy so strong, that he decided to retreat to Wills Creek, Cumberland, Maryland, where her could reinforce his army. The French continued to advance rapidly. Washington had to shorten his retreat, and encamped at Fort Necessity.

On July 3, 1754, late in the morning, de Villiers reached Fort Necessity. He began an attack immediately. After about nine hours of fighting, both forces had almost exhausted their ammunition. De Villiers demanded a surrender. The next morning, July 4, Washington accepted de Villeir's proposal and signed a paper of surrender. Washington, who did not know French, was unaware that the document he signed was an admission that he had *assassinated* Jumonville. This inadvertent admission was later to be an embarrassment to Washington, and an incentive to the French soldiers to continue their fight against the English.[17]

To compensate for the defeat at Fort Necessity, General Edward Braddock, a more experienced soldier who was in command of all English forces in America, determined that he would lead an army of more than 2,000 men to drive the French from Fort Duquesne. On June 10, 1755, the British army began a long, slow back-breaking march through the mountains of Pennsylvania. By July 8, however, they were within ten miles of Fort Duquesne.

The French were aware that they could not defend Fort Duquesne against such a large force of soldiers and artillery. Using guerilla tactics in a heavily wooded area, a small army under the command of Leonard Daniel de Beaujeau made a shambles of Braddock's much larger force. Beaujeau was killed. Braddock, who was mortally wounded, died as his defeated army retreated. To hide his grave, his body was buried in the middle of the road, about one mile from Fort Necessity. This encounter is noted in history as "Braddock's Defeat."

These disastrous defeats strengthened England's determination to reclaim control over western Pennsylvania, by a conquest of Fort Duquesne. It took three years to plan and organize the sufficient troops, weapons and supplies for this important campaign. General John Forbes was placed in command of this military force.

In September 1758, as General Forbes's army was progressing toward Fort Duquesne, an advance contingent of 800 Highlanders, under the charge of an ambitious young officer, Major James Grant, reached a hill within sight of Fort Duquesne. Grant's dream of an unauthorized personal conquest was shattered as he led his men into a guerilla-type trap by French and Native American soldiers. His valiant warriors were decimated. The location of this battle would later be known as Grant's Hill.[18]

General Forbes was more cautious and deliberate as he approached Fort Duquesne. But caution was no longer necessary. As Forbes entered the area on November 24, 1758, he found that Fort Duquesne had been deserted and burned. A lack of supplies had forced the French garrison to withdraw.

Fort Pitt rose over the ashes of Fort Duquesne. Larger than its predecessor, Fort Pitt shares the same location. A remnant block house of this fort survives. On January 21, 1759, General Forbes named the area "Pittsburgh" in honor of the Prime Minister of England, William Pitt.[19]

For the next 50 years, following the departure of the French, there was no official resident priest in Pittsburgh. Catholics living in western Pennsylvania had no means to publicly practice their faith.

Ecclesiastical jurisdiction changed with the change of government. From 1534 when Jacques Cartier claimed this hemisphere for France, Catholics were under the ecclesiastical jurisdiction of the bishop of Quebec. With Britain in control, this jurisdiction passed from Bishop Henri-Marie de Pontbriand of Quebec to Bishop Richard Challoner, the vicar-apostolic of London.

For many years the only priests to visit Pittsburgh and vicinity were those who were passing through to assignments farther west.[20] Among these were Frs. Benedict J. Flaget, Simon Brute, and Deacon Stephen

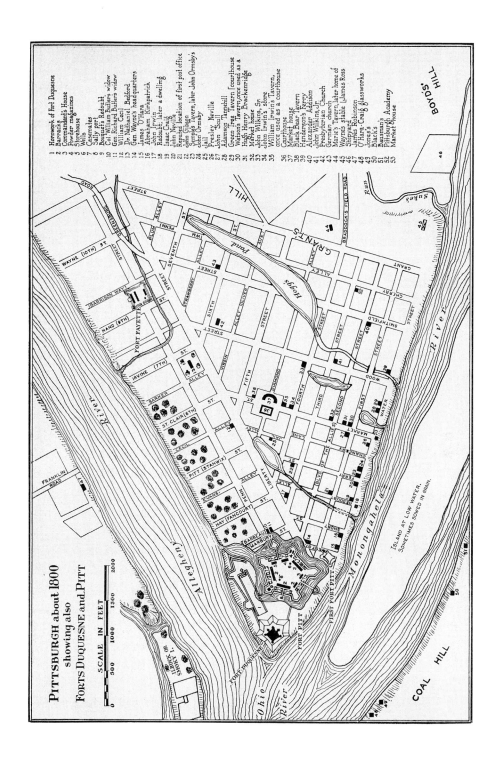

1 Hornwork of Fort Duquesne
2 Barracks
3 Commandant's House
4 Powder magazines
5 Storehouse
6 Wells
7 Casemates
8 Sally port
9 Bouquet's Redoubt
10 Col. William Butler's widow
11 Gen. Richard Butler's widow
12 William Cecil
13 Dr. Nathaniel Bedford
14 Gen. Wayne's headquarters
15 James O'Hara
16 Abraham Kirkpatrick
17 John Irwin
18 Redoubt, later a dwelling
19 Isaac Craig
20 John Neville
21 Reputed location of first post office
22 John Gibson
23 Semple's tavern, later John Ormsby's
24 John Ormsby
25 Jail
26 Presley Neville
27 John Scull
28 Adamson Tannehill
29 Green Free Tavern [courthouse
30 Watson's Tavern,once used as a
31 High Henry Brackenridge
32 Market house
33 John Wilkins, Sr.
34 John Irwin's store
35 William Irwin's Tavern,
   once used as a courthouse
36 Courthouse
37 Market house
38 Black Bear Tavern
39 Henderson's Ferry
40 Alexander Addison
41 John Wilkins,Jr.
42 Presbyterian Church
43 German church
44 Marie's Tavern, later home of
45 Wayne's stable [James Ross
46 Shipyard
47 James Robinson
48 O'Hara-Craig glassworks
49 Jones's
50 Black's
51 Bausman's
52 Pittsburgh Academy
53 Market house

PITTSBURGH about 1800
showing also
FORTS DUQUESNE and PITT

T. Badin, all exiles from the French Revolution. That upheaval forced them to emigrate, in 1792, to the United States, where they offered their services to Bp. John Carroll.

Badin had refused ordination from the bishop of Orleans because the bishop had not resisted the new revolutionary government in France. Fr. Badin was Bp. Carroll's first ordinand and the first priest ordained in the United States.

The most notable of these men was the Sulpician Fr. Benedict J. Flaget, born in Conteynat, near Billour, Auvergne, France, on November 1, 1763. After his studies and preparation for the priesthood — at the Sulpician seminary at Clermont — he was ordained in 1787 at Issy, France. Flaget arrived in America on March 29, 1792, and was assigned to Fort Vincennes in Indiana. Fr. Flaget, who had expected to teach in a seminary, spent his American years as an active missionary priest and bishop.

In May 1792, he began a six-month stay in Pittsburgh. During this period, Fr. Flaget worked indefatigably during a smallpox epidemic. At the same time, General Anthony Wayne prepared his army for an expedition against the Native Americans. While both men were in Pittsburgh, Wayne became a friend and admirer of Fr. Flaget. The depth of this friendship is illustrated by an unusual incident. While they were in training, four soldiers of Wayne's army defected. Two were Catholics, one a Protestant, and the other a French atheist. They were captured and sentenced to death. Fr. Flaget visited them in prison. He reconciled the Catholics and converted the Protestant. The French atheist was obdurate. Fr. Flaget was so affected by the thought that his countryman was going to die unrepentant that General Wayne commuted the man's sentence and put the other three to death.

In 1808, Fr. Flaget became the first bishop of Bardstown, Kentucky. He died in Louisville, Kentucky, on February 11, 1850.[21]

Two

Religious Freedom

Congress shall pass no law respecting the establishment of religion, or prohibiting the exercise thereof.
              First Amendment, Constitution of the United States

In colonial times, to be known as a Catholic meant a most difficult and despised life. The majority of the English-speaking population was not Catholic, and the established religion of each colony was a strongly anti-Catholic Church.

The paramount impetus for immigration to the United States was to avoid religious persecution, for both Catholics and non-Catholics. Most of the non-Catholics settled in New England, and soon they reenacted the proscriptive laws of England which denied Catholics the right to vote or to own property.

To establish an asylum where Catholics could live without persecution, George Calvert, First Lord Baltimore, obtained from King James I, a tract of land south of Pennsylvania, which he called "Maryland." George Calvert died before he could accomplish his desire, but his son, Cecil Calvert, Second Lord Baltimore, organized a colony which sailed to America in the ships, "The Ark" and "The Dove" in 1633. Leonard Calvert served as the Governor of Maryland. Their goal was to establish a refuge where "no Christian should be compelled to worship contrary to his conscience."

Lord Baltimore's dream of religious freedom was a noble but fragile ideal. His freedom of worship for all people allowed an influx of Puritans into Maryland. Eventually the Puritans became dominant in

13

the Maryland assembly, assumed control of the colony, and then proscribed the Catholic Religion.[1]

This renewal of persecution precipitated an exodus of Catholics from Maryland. Many sought refuge in Pennsylvania where freedom of worship was protected by William Penn's Quakers. Since they were tolerated, a colony of Catholics settled in eastern Pennsylvania and became the forefathers of those who later moved to western Pennsylvania — to the Diocese of Pittsburgh.

The American Revolution was a catalyst in the emancipation of religious worship, and in the establishment of the American hierarchy. At the outbreak of the war, Catholics were generally suspected of Tory sympathies by other colonists. This attitude grew, stimulated by the passage of the Quebec Act, which granted religious freedom to Catholics in Canada and in the Ohio and Mississippi valleys. Most of the colonists of New England resented this law, and it became the spark which ignited active opposition to the English government.[2]

As the war progressed, the invaluable aid and cooperation by Catholic leaders such as the Marquis de Lafayette, Admiral Rochambeau, engineer Thaddeus Kosiusko, cavalry officer Casimir Pulaski, and Navy Captain John Barry, contributed to the success of the American forces. Religious restrictions were swept aside. Opposition to Catholics diminished, as independence guaranteed religious freedom.

Even President Washington appreciated the patriotism of Catholics, as evidenced by a letter he wrote after his inauguration.

March 12, 1790

To the Catholics of America:

    I presume that your fellow citizens will not forget the patriotic part which you took in the accomplishment of their Revolution, and the establishment of their Government—or the important assistance which they received from a nation in which the Roman Catholic faith is professed.

(Signed)   George Washington[3]

That "all men are created equal" was a practical demand for freedom of religious worship. At the first Congress of the Federal Government in December 1791, diplomats from Maryland, drawing on their own experiences, supported adoption of the Bill of Rights, especially the First Amendment, which guarantees freedom of religion. The sixth article of the Constitution had already disallowed any "religious test" as a qualification for "any office or public trust." Theoretically, Catholics were to be considered equal with all other citizens.

SEPARATION OF CHURCH AND STATE

"Separation of Church and State," a remark made by President Thomas Jefferson in a letter to Danbury Baptists, in 1802, was adopted as the official interpretation of the First Amendment to the Constitution of the Untied States. Jefferson wrote:

> Religion is a matter which lies solely between man and his God. I contemplate with sovereign reverence that act of the whole American people which declared that their legislature should make no law respecting the establishment of religion or prohibiting the free exercise thereof, thus building a wall of separation between Church and State.

In 1803, Jefferson proposed a $100 subsidy for a chaplain for the Kaskasia Indians and $300 for the erection of a church.

That same year, the United States Government acquired the Louisiana territory, and the superior of the Ursuline Convent in New Orleans wrote to President Jefferson inquiring about the convent's status in the light of the Louisiana Purchase. The man who has a reputation of being somewhat irreligious wrote this reply:

> I have received, Holy Sisters, the letters you have written to me, wherein you express anxiety for the property vested in your institutions by the former Government of Louisiana. The principles of the Constitution of the United States are a sure guaranty to you that it will be preserved to you sacred and inviolate, and that your institution will be permitted to govern itself according to its voluntary rules, without interference from the civil authority. Whatever diversity of shade may appear in the religious opinions of our fellow citizens, the charitable objects of your institution cannot be indifferent to any, and its furtherance of the wholesome purposes of training up its young members in the way they should go, cannot fail to insure it the patronage of the government it is under. Be assured it will meet with all the protection my office can give it.
> I salute you, Holy Sisters, with friendship and respect.
> Thomas Jefferson[4]

AMERICAN HIERARCHY

Two more events helped lay a strong and faithful foundation for the future Diocese of Pittsburgh: the formation of the Church hierarchy in the United States and settlement of Catholic families in western Pennsylvania.

The Carroll family, which played an important role in the foundation of the American nation, also played an indispensable part in the foundation of the American Catholic Church. Charles Carroll of Carrollton signed the Declaration of Independence, and his cousin, Daniel Carroll, helped to compose the Constitution and the Bill of Rights. Fr. John Carroll, Daniel's brother, became the first Bishop in the United States.

At the outbreak of the Revolution, Catholics in the eastern colonies were subjects of Bp. Challoner, the vicar-apostolic of London, and his vicar in the western hemisphere, Fr. John Lewis.

At the war's conclusion in 1783, the American clergy appealed to the Vatican for a change of supervision because apparent subjection to an English hierarchy would not please the American Continental Congress. One year later, Fr. John Carroll was named by Pope Pius VI to be provisional superior of the American Catholic missions, with the right to confer the Sacrament of Confirmation. Fr. Carroll accepted this appointment as prefect-apostolic on February 27, 1785.

A prefect-apostolic was an asset in the administration of ecclesiastical affairs, but there was a real need for a bishop. On March 12, 1788, the clergy of America requested the privilege of electing their first bishop. The Vatican agreed. This was a singular exemption, granted to avoid any criticism by the American public of foreign domination. In an election conducted during April 1789, Fr. John Carroll received 24 of the 26 votes. On November 16, 1789, the pope appointed Fr. John Carroll to be the Bishop of all the territories of the United States. Bp. Carroll chose Baltimore for his See.

When Bp. Carroll accepted the office, there were 24 priests caring for 30,000 Catholics in the United States.

It was a remarkable coincidence that the first Bishop of the United States assumed his duties in the same year as the first President of the United States. President Washington and Bp. Carroll have often been compared because they possessed many identical qualities.

JOHN CARROLL

John Carroll was born in Upper Marlboro, Maryland, in 1735, and he received his early education in a small Jesuit School at Bohemia Manor, Maryland. To obtain further education, he had to go to Europe. He and his older brother Daniel sailed for France in 1748.

While a student at the Jesuit School of St. Omer in northern France, he applied to join the Society of Jesus and was ordained in 1761. He became a professor in the College of Liege, France.

Eight years after his ordination, the Jesuits were suppressed. Acting on his own, Fr. Carroll returned to Maryland and began an active life as a missionary priest. He was soon a leader of the American clergy.

At the outbreak of the American Revolutionary War, he was sent as an advisor with a diplomatic delegation to Canada. His cousin Charles Carroll, Benjamin Franklin, and Daniel Chase formed the delegation. Fr. Carroll and Benjamin Franklin developed a firm friendship on the trip, but the delegation was unsuccessful in persuading Canada to become an American ally.

When Franklin was the ambassador to France, he served as an intermediary between Fr. Carroll and the Vatican. He also shuttled between the Vatican and the United States Government. Through Franklin, the Vatican requested the nomination of a bishop, as it was compelled to do with many governments in Europe. The United States Congress responded that ecclesiastical appointments were not their concern.

Bp. Carroll was very solicitous for the welfare of his subjects. He made many endeavors to obtain priests to meet their needs. When, in 1792, Sulpician priests came from France, this enabled him to establish a seminary in Baltimore, and also to send some of these priests into mission territories. Assured of the necessity of higher education, Bp. Carroll founded the school which is now Georgetown University. He was also a firm support to Saint Elizabeth Ann Seton, and assisted her in founding her school and her religious community, the American Sisters of Charity.

Bp. Carroll believed it was his duty to build and adapt a church in conformity with the ideals of freedom in America. He found no problem in giving religious obedience to the pope while reserving civil obedience to the secular state. The manner and policies of Bp. Carroll did much to bring about a remarkable period of religious harmony in the new American republic. The persecutions and suspicions of past generations were being set aside. Catholics were slowly accepted as full and respected citizens of their country.[5]

John Carroll had been Archbishop of Baltimore for 25 years when he died on December 3, 1815, in his 81st year. He had succeeded in putting the Church in America on a firm foundation.

Three

Catholic Pioneers in Western Pennsylvania

As Catholic families moved from Maryland into Pennsylvania, the chapel at Conewago, near Gettysburg, became the cradle of Catholicism in the state. The Conewago settlement was orginally founded as a refuge for English-speaking Catholics, but as emigration from Europe increased, many Germans were welcomed into the colony. The parish at Conewago extended to the western border of Pennsylvania and was the base of operations for priests assigned to serve the state's western counties.

In 1784, Felix Hughes of Waynesburg delivered a petition to Father Ferdinand Farmer, who passed it on to Fr. John Carroll, at that time the Superior of the Missions of North America. This petition, signed by 73 Catholics, requested that a priest come to western Pennsylvania "once a year." Unfortunately, Fr. Carroll was unable to grant this simple request.[1]

In that same year, Arthur Lee, who had served with Benjamin Franklin at the court of Versailles, was a visitor in Pittsburgh. On December 24, 1784, he wrote in his observations of the city that there was "no priest of any persuasion" in the locality.[2]

Less than two years passed before six families, in anticipation of a priest being assigned to their district, bought one acre of land in Greensburg. They began constructing a log church, but it was never completed. That property is now the site of Blessed Sacrament Cathedral, Greensburg.

In June, 1789, Fr. John B. Cause, O.F.M., an itinerant priest who "spoke English middling well and some French" did stop in Westmoreland County. Fr. Cause was not officially appointed to the area, and although he knew the families' needs, he did not remain with them.[3] Soon after Fr. Cause abandoned this group of farmers, Fr. Theodore Brouwers, O.F.M., was assigned, in 1793, to form a parish in Westmoreland County.

Fr. Brouwers was born in Rotterdam, Holland, in 1738. He was ordained a priest on June 5, 1767, in Mechlin. After ordination, he taught philosophy and theology in Brussells, Belgium. In 1776 he was appointed vicar-apostolic in Curacao and given charge of all missionaries in the West Indies.

One year later, Brouwers came to Philadelphia and in 1790 applied for the Westmoreland County parish. Fr. Brouwers knew his prospective parishioners were poor and was well aware of the dangers of trusteeism. Before leaving on his journey into Westmoreland County, he purchased 315 acres of land in Derry Township, near New Alexandria. When Fr. Brouwers arrived at this newly purchased property, he realized that it was too far from the residences of his parishioners. He was advised to purchase Sportsman's Hall, a 300-acre tract in Beatty Township, near Latrobe, which is now the site of St. Vincent Archabbey and College. He immediately began to organize a parish, which for the next 18 years became the center of Catholic worship in western Pennsylvania.

Ill health shortened his life and Fr. Brouwers died on October 29, 1790. At his death, he was 53 years old, 29 years a priest. He had been pastor at Sportsman's Hall for only seven months.

Fr. Brouwers's tenure had been short, but litigation over his will lasted for five years. In the hope of encouraging a priest to accept his parish, he bestowed all his possessions "to a Roman Catholic Priest that shall succeed me in this place."[4] Contrary to Fr. Brouwers's desires, his proposal resulted in unworthy applicants for that parish. When Fr. Cause learned of the bequest, he returned to Greensburg and claimed the pastorate and the properties. In a very short time he went to Philadelphia and unlawfully withdrew money from Brouwers's account, which he appropriated to his own use. Cause was soon suspended and excommunicated by Fr. Carroll for these illegal actions.

On May 2, 1791, Fr. Francis Fromm, O.F.M. who had learned the

ST. VINCENT COLLEGE.   BEATTY, PA.
SPORTMAN'S HALL, ST. VINCENT'S IN 1789.

Sportsman's Hall, on what is now the site of St. Vincent Archabbey at Latrobe, served as the center of Catholic worship in western Pennsylvania for nearly two decades beginning in 1790.

details of Brouwers's will from Fr. Cause, arrived at Sportsman's Hall without official approval. Because of disagreements with parishioners, Fr. Fromm had recently been removed from a parish in Lancaster. He soon persuaded the parishioners of Sportsman's Hall to elect him as their pastor. He then laid claim to what remained of Fr. Brouwers's estate.

Amid charges of misconduct, Fr. Fromm's faculties were revoked on May 17, 1793. The next year his parishioners demanded that he reconcile with Bishop Carroll or leave the parish. On August 5, 1795, Fr. Fromm was forbidden to celebrate Mass because he had "never been commisioned to exercise pastoral functions" at Sportsman's Hall.[5]

Despite this lack of official standing, Fromm sued Bp. Carroll and the parish in an effort to enforce his claim of ownership of Sportsman's Hall. This litigation resulted in a landmark decision when Judge Alexander Addison of Westmoreland County supported the authority of the Roman Catholic Bishop in his civil court ruling against Fr.

21

Fromm.[6] Fromm fell victim to the yellow fever plague, dying in 1799.

After Fr. Fromm's expulsion in 1795, the difficult task of leading the parish at Sportsman's Hall was assigned to Fr. Lawrence Phelan, O.F.M. Cap. The outrageous behavior of the last two priests had damaged parish morale. The parishioners who remained were divided into factions, and the formidable task of reorganization was aggravated by deplorable living conditions. On October 17, 1795, Fr. Phelan wrote to Bp. Carroll complaining that the bishop had "no conception of my distress here."[7] Soon after this letter, Phelan left this assignment. He was stationed at Buffalo Creek in 1805 and moved to Chambersburg in 1807. He returned to Ireland in 1811 and died in Dublin in 1824.

Fr. Patrick Lonergan, O.F.M., succeeded Phelan at Sportsman's Hall. Even though he was an energetic priest, Lonergan also left the parish after a short time. He began a parish in West Alexander in Washington County, but this venture was unsuccessful as well. He then transferred to Waynesburg, Greene County, where he remained until 1805. From Waynesburg, Fr. Lonergan went to New Orleans.

DEMETRIUS A. GALLITZIN

Captain Michael McGuire, Jr., descendant of a Catholic family that migrated from Maryland to eastern Pennsylvania, was a soldier and a farmer. In August of 1775, he served in the Massachusetts militia under Captain Michael Cresap. In 1776, he recruited and commanded a Frederick County, Maryland, militia in the Revolutionary War. In 1785, he moved his family to a hunting camp in the Allegheny mountains of Cambria County, Pennsylvania. He had purchased this land in 1768.

Friends and relatives followed Michael McGuire into Cambria county and formed the McGuire Settlement. McGuire, who hoped that a priest would be assigned to his settlement, sent aside 60 acres for a chapel and graveyard.

This priestless colony became the stage for one of the most dramatic episodes in the story of western Pennsylvania Catholicism. In October, 1795, the wife of John Burgoon, a resident of the settlement, became gravely ill. She expressed her wish to become a Catholic and receive the Sacraments.

The nearest priest was at Conewago, 150 miles to the east. Undaunted by the rough mountain terrain, Mrs. Luke McGuire and a female companion made the arduous trip to Conewago on horseback. They explained the purpose of their journey and begged that a priest accompany them back to their homes so that Mrs. Burgoon's desires could be fulfilled.

A young priest, Fr. Demetrius A. Gallitzin — the first priest to receive all his seminary education and formation in the United States — responded. To conceal the nobility of his family background — his father was the Russian Prince Demetrius and his mother, Countess Amalia, was the daughter of a Prussian field marshall — he was known as Augustine Smith. During his visit, Fr. Gallitzin was attracted to the beauty of the McGuire Settlement and the warmth of its people. He administered the sacraments to Mrs. Burgoon, celebrated Mass and gave pastoral assistance to all Catholics in the area. Gallitzin was also quick to recognize the needs of the mountain settlers, who had retained a strong faith despite the absence of a priest.

Fr. Gallitzin returned to Conewago and was assigned to a little church at Taneytown, Maryland. The trustees of this parish, in the heady sense of democratic freedom common immediately after the Revolutionary War, made life miserable for the young priest, as they thought their office gave them complete control of the parish.

During this time, Fr. Gallitzin again visited the McGuire Settlement. The people there were eager for him to remain, and he wished to serve them. Residents of the settlement wrote to Bp. Carroll and asked that Gallitzin be appointed their pastor. Fr. Gallitzin himself also wrote the bishop, expressing his willingness to accept the assignment. Bp. Carroll, concerned that western Pennsylvania Catholics were being neglected, knew that stationing a priest in the Allegheny Mountains would be a partial solution to the problem.

Bp. Carroll granted the request on March 1, 1799, but Fr. Gallitzin could not arrange to leave Taneytown until October. That month, equipped with the many necessities required for life in an isolated region, Gallitzin drove a prairie schooner to his new assignment.

At the McGuire Settlement, construction of a log church, the only Catholic church between Lancaster, Pennsylvania and St. Louis, Missouri, began immediately. Erection of the building progressed so quickly that the house of prayer was ready for Midnight Mass on Christmas Day, 1799.

Father Demetrius Gallitzin, the first priest to receive all his seminary education in the United States, began serving Catholics in western Pennsylvania in 1799 near present-day Loretto.

Gallitzin was on his way to fulfilling his dream: forming an ideal Catholic frontier settlement. Within one year of his arrival, he established Saint Michael School, the first parochial school in western Pennsylvania. Archibald Christy was the first teacher. His duties were later assumed by Franciscan Brothers and Sisters of Mercy.[8]

At this time, McGuire Settlement was just a collection of farms. Gallitzin was convinced that a town would facilitate commerce. He mapped out a village on his own property and named the town "Loretto" after the shrine of Our Lady in Italy.

Fr. Gallitzin had been receiving subsidies from his wealthy Russian family, but because of the Napoleonic wars and British blockades, their assistance became more and more irregular. After his mother's death in 1806, the payments ceased. In his zeal to expand the church and the town, Fr. Gallitzin had overextended himself financially. For the first time in his life, he was in debt and dependent on some friends for assistance.

Missionary life was never serene or without problems. Besides the imposed rustic lifestyle and his financial woes, Gallitzin had to contend with rebellious newcomers to the parish who were outspoken in their opposition to his autocratic management and discipline. They even disapproved of his political allegiance to the Federalist party. Though they constituted a small minority of the parishioners, these individuals were vocal, and they resorted to false accusations and slanderous statements about their pastor.[9]

In a letter to Bp. Carroll on May 11, 1807, Fr. Gallitzin wrote "I am completely innocent in all those cases in which I am accused.[10]

When the defamers forwarded their complaints to Bp. Carroll, they received a reprimand for their calumnies and insurbordination.

Fr. Gallitzin was seriously disturbed by these controversies and was very unhappy that he should be misunderstood and slandered. For some time he ignored their accusations, but eventually he had to denounce his detractors. This induced his critics to retract their slanderous remarks, and he emerged from the controversy with greater esteem and influence.[11]

At times, Gallitzin also had to be an apologist for the faith. On one occasion he defended Catholicism against a vicious sermon that had been reprinted in the *Huntington Gazette*. His response was later published in a book titled *A Defense of Catholic Principles*.

For many of his years at Loretto, Gallitzin served as vicar-general of the Diocese of Philadelphia. He was the bishop's representative for the western part of the state and was well acquainted with the growth and expanse of the diocese. In 1823, he wrote to Archbishop Ambrose Marechal of Baltimore, recommending Loretto as a good site for the diocese needed in western Pennsylvania.

Though his recommendation of Loretto was not accepted, Fr. Gallitzin himself was proposed for episcopal appointments. He always declined such nominations.[12]

The winter of 1839–1840 was unusually hard on the aging priest. A fall from his horse left him crippled and unable to ride, but he designed a sleigh in which he could continue his parochial obligation. After the liturgies of Holy Week and Easter, Fr. Gallitzin was unable to get out of bed on Easter Monday. He was seriously ill. On May 6, 1840, Fr. Gallitzin died. He is buried in his beloved Loretto.

Fr. Gallitzin's legacy was an example of dedication to God, pastoral work and to his parishioners. The strict discipline he learned as a young man — for a time he was aide-de-camp to Austrian General von Lillien — greatly influenced his pastoral style. The sign he placed in the vestibule of his Loretto church is a classic example of his autocratic approach:

1. Scrape the dirt off your shoes on the iron scraper provided for that purpose.
2. Do not spit on the floor of the Chapel.
3. Do not put your hats and caps on the Chapel windows.
4. Do not rub against the papered walls of the Chapel.
5. Do not put your heels on the washboards.
6. After coming in at the passage door, shut the door after you.[13]

Admiration for the life and work of Fr. Demetrius A. Gallitzin is not limited to the Church he served so long and so well. The Commonwealth of Pennsylvania commemorated his achievements by naming a public park — the Prince Gallitzin State Park, located in northeastern Cambria County — in his honor.

PETER HELBRON, O.F.M. Cap.

The year 1799 was an auspicious one for Catholics in western Pennsylvania. One month after Fr. Gallitzin arrived at the McGuire Settlement as the first resident priest in the western part of the state, the Capuchin Friar Peter Helbron came to the parish of Sportsman's Hall.

Fr. Helbron was "a man of culture and refinement."[14] Having served as an expert horseman in the Prussian army, he maintained a meticulously neat appearance. Exuding a commanding presence, Fr. Helbron suffused the performance of his priestly duties with real dignity.

Peter Helbron and his brother, Fr. Charles Helbron, also a Capuchin Franciscan, arrived in Philadelphia on October 14, 1787. They came in response to a request for German priests to work among the German immigrants.

Charles Helbron endured an unpleasant tenure at Holy Trinity Church, Philadelphia, due to conflicts with church trustees over administration of parish finances. Again, the trustees' new sense of Americanism and democracy was often at odds with the priest's responsibilities. The trustees also claimed the right to name pastors and assistants. Because of these conflicts, Fr. Charles returned to Germany in 1791. On November 25, 1793, a victim of the French Revolution, Charles Helbron was guillotined in Bayonne, France.

As incredible as it seems, Peter Helbron was chosen to succeed his brother, Fr. Charles, as pastor of Holy Trinity. Normalcy reigned for five years but the problems of trusteeism eventually forced Fr. Helbron to leave the parish as well. He transferred to St. Joseph Church in Philadelphia in 1796.

Three years later, on November 17, 1799, Fr. Helbron assumed the pastorate at Sportsman's Hall. There he inherited the problems created by Fr. Francis Fromm, but he soon acquired title to the properties and began reorganizing the parish. He quickly became acquainted with the people and their needs. His firm but gentle kindness won the admiration of his parishioners and gained their support and cooperation. The congregation built a house both as his residence and their place of worship. Fr. Helbron blessed this building as a church and dedicated it as the Chapel of the Holy Cross. The chapel served well for 10 years. When it became inadequate, the parishioners built a larger church.[15]

At Sportsman's Hall the congregation expected Fr. Peter Helbron to live as a farmer and did not give him a salary. But farming was not his forte, and he was forced to appeal for assistance.

Fr. Helbron's parish included all the land west of the Allegheny Mountains and from the Mason-Dixon Line in the south to Lake Erie in the north. The Capuchin friar made periodic visits throughout the area, especially to the missions at Brownsville, Sugar Creek and Pittsburgh.[16]

Trained to be methodical and careful, Helbron kept records of baptisms, marriages and funerals, and they are a source of valuable information on the members of the Sportsman's Hall congregation and also on the missionary visits throughout western Pennsylvania.

Fr. Helbron was responsible for beginning a church in Pittsburgh. He wrote to Bp. Carroll on November 22, 1806, stating that a Colonel James O'Hara had presented a "fine lot" to him on which he was to build a Catholic church, and that $1,000 had been collected for that purpose.[17]

Fr. Helbron, in his sixties, and Fr. Gallitzin, in his thirties, were the only resident priests in the western half of the state. They became very close friends who worked for and depended on each other. This mutual friendship and cooperation was a great asset to the development of the Church in western Pennsylvania.

In 1811, Fr. Helbron's health began to fail. A tumor developed on his neck which local physicians, over a period of five years, were unable to treat. In 1816, Helbron underwent neck surgery in Philadelphia, but the doctors were unsuccessful. Wishing to die in his beloved parish, he began the journey to Sportsman's Hall. Arriving at Carlisle, Pennsylvania, he was too weak to continue on the trip. He died on April 24, 1816, and was buried near St. Patrick Church.[18]

A biographer of Fr. Helbron's life, Benedictine Fr. Gerard Bridge, summarizes his accomplishments at Sportsman's Hall:

> The works that he left behind during the sixteen years of his ministry: his zeal in the care of souls: his arduous labors for the spread of God's kingdom; the fidelity with which he served the people, and the love which he constantly manifested towards the lowest of his flock: these are the stones in the monument which he erected with his own hands and by which a grateful people hold his memory in loving remembrance and lasting benediction.[19]

THE SUGAR CREEK MISSION

Religious persecution and financial hardships drove many people to seek a better life in America. On June 4, 1792 a group of emigrants from County Donegal, Ireland, set sail for New York. Jerry Monaghan, a poet among the passengers on the brig *Eliza*, wrote a song describing the voyage as very slow and stormy. The bad weather blew their two-masted vessel off course and they landed at New Castle, Delaware, on September 9.

Most of the Irish emigrants followed Braddock's trail and headed for western Pennsylvania. The Treaty of Fort McIntosh, signed on January 21, 1785, had ordered Native American tribes to withdraw from Pennsylvania. But skirmishes between them and the white settlers continued. As a result, the former Donegal Colony residents settled at Indian Creek near Connellsville.

Nine years later, in August 1794, General Anthony Wayne defeated the tribes in the Battle of the Maumee in Ohio. Two years after that victory, in 1796, the Donegal Colony moved north and established a permanent settlement in Buffalo Creek or Sugar Creek, at the border of Armstrong and Butler counties. The Donegal colonists were Catholic farmers. They had a simplicity and fervor of faith that drew compliments from the priests who served them.

Fr. Patrick Lonergan visited the colony in 1801, and Fr. Helbron was there in 1803. In 1805, Fr. Lawrence Phelan, who had left Sportsman's Hall because of the disruptive situation created by Frs. Cause and Fromm, took up residence with the Donegal Colony. The parishioners built a church and rectory, and Fr. Phelan remained with these people for five years.

In his *History of the Dioceses of Pittsburgh and Allegheny*, Msgr. Andrew A. Lambing relates inspiring anecdotes about the settlers at Sugar Creek. Lambing admired their devotion to the faith as well as their ingenious work ethic. Lack of funds did not stop the settlers from constructing their church. The section of the building on which a person worked was determined by the location of one's home in relation to the church. The parish was divided into four sections, each under the control of a parishioner. The men of the community were accustomed to helping their neighbors erect barns, and they planned to build their church in the same way. A date was set to meet at the site, but a shortage of nails postponed the completion of the roof until the following year, 1806, when the church was named for Ireland's patron, St. Patrick.[20]

Phelan's departure in 1810 left the Donegal Colony without a resident priest until Fr. Charles Ferry arrived in 1821. He remained at St. Patrick's for five years. When there was no resident priest at Sugar Creek, priests from Pittsburgh and Sportsman's Hall visited periodically.

Fr. Patrick O'Neill, the first resident pastor at St. Mary Church in Freeport, cared for St. Patrick's as a mission from 1826 until 1833. Fr. O'Neill and his parishioners were great apologists for and defenders of the faith. In 1831, O'Neill published a pamphlet: *A Sermon on the Mystery of the Real Presence, Preached in the Court House in the Borough of Butler.* His talk was a rebuttal to a sermon preached by the Rev. Issac Noblock. Tradition relates that Bp. Kenrick had to tone down Fr. O'Neill's response. When Fr. O'Neill departed from Freeport, because of failing health, he left the Diocese of Pittsburgh. He was working in Chicago at the time of his death, June 15, 1879.

One year after O'Neill's departure, Bp. Kenrick and Fr. Masquelet visited Sugar Creek in the summer of 1834. Kenrick described the religious devotion he witnessed amid the hardships of the frontier:

> The church of St. Patrick, Buffalo Creek, Armstrong County, was next visited. This congregation is also destitute of a pastor. The church is of unwrought wood, and might vie with the apostolic times for unadorned plainness and simplicity. During five days, from Thursday until the following Tuesday, (May 15–20, 1834), from 5 or 6 o'clock until 6 or 7 in the evening, the confessional was crowded with penitents. Many of them had come great distances and remained fasting until a late hour in the day. Among these was an old lady who, although in her eightieth year, had walked a mile and a half to be present at the Holy Sacrifice and eat that Flesh which was given for the life of the world. About 300 received Holy Communion, and Confirmation was given to 90 persons, some of whom had travelled 50 miles to receive this gift of the Holy Ghost. The scenes exhibited during these five days were similar to those which excited the Saviour's compassion over the neglected people, who were as sheep wandering without a shepherd and necessarily brought to mind His command to the Apostles, to pray to the Lord of the harvest, that He would send laborers into the harvest.[21]

JAMES O'HARA

James O'Hara, one of the most successful businessmen in the post-Revolutionary War period, was born in Ireland in 1754. He immigrated to America before the outbreak of the war and served in the Continental Army. After the war, O'Hara came to Pittsburgh. He was well educated and became a clerk in the surveying firm of Simon and Campbell.

Soon afterward, he became a partner with two traders, Devereaux Smith and Ephraim Douglass. By 1784, O'Hara was Quartermaster-General, giving him responsibility for supplying the western forces of the United States Army. He also became well acquainted with the needs of people and learned how to transport all types of necessities.

O'Hara was a real entrepreneur. Gifted with intelligence and sound judgment, he started businesses and operated them with aplomb. He owned a retail store, a brewery, a sawmill, a tannery, and a gristmill. With Isaac Craig, O'Hara established a window glass and bottle factory in 1797. In addition to interests in ship building, O'Hara owned hugh parcels of real estate.[22]

James O'Hara was an outstanding leader in the community and his name appears on almost every civic list of the era. He even ventured into politics, but that proved unsuccessful. In 1804, Pressley Neville defeated O'Hara in the race for Burgess of Pittsburgh.

O'Hara was a staunch Catholic at a time when Pittsburgh was considered a Presbyterian community. While he had married a Presbyterian and supported the First Presbyterian Church, James O'Hara still favored his Catholic faith. His home at Short and Water streets, near the Monongahela River, contained a priest's room where visiting clergy could lodge and offer Mass.

In 1806, O'Hara and his wife, Mary, donated a parcel of land at Liberty and Washington streets as a site for the future St. Patrick Church which became the predecessor of Old St. Patrick Church.

Although he attended the Presbyterian Church, O'Hara retained his Catholic faith. In 1819, when he was dying and no priest was available, he had a servant read the *Prayer for the Dying* from his Catholic prayer book.

Two of James O'Hara's granchildren made notable contributions to the history of Pittsburgh.

On October 3, 1889, a granddaughter, Mary Groghan — whose marriage to Capt. Edward Schenley on February 14, 1842, was the romance of the century — bequeathed 300 acres that she had inherited to the City of Pittsburgh to be used as a public park. Schenley Park, in the Oakland section of the city, the city's first public park, is a memorial to her donation. In 1905, the city provided a portion of this property as a site for the present Carnegie Mellon University.

A grandson, Harmar Denny, was a student for the Episcopal priesthood who converted to Roman Catholicism. He was ordained a priest and later became a Jesuit. He was nationally noted as a lecturer and was a popular retreat director.

WILLIAM F. X. O'BRIEN

Pittsburgh was still a mission of the Sportsman's Hall parish when Fr. William F. X. O'Brien was assigned there in 1808, the first resident pastor in Pittsburgh.

Fr. O'Brien was born in Maryland and prepared for the priesthood there. Ordained by Bp. Carroll on April 11, 1808, he arrived in Pittsburgh in November of that year.

A brick church was under construction on the site donated by James O'Hara. Progress on the church was slow because the parishioners were poor. Even when the church was dedicated by Bp. Egan in August 1811, there were no pews. A plan was devised so that each person who wanted a pew would mark their desired spot on the floor. When they could afford it, they would ask a carpenter to make a pew for them.

Despite the lack of funds, Fr. O'Brien procured a pipe organ in 1812. He was severely criticized by parishioners for this unnecessary extravagance.

When Fr. Helbron died in 1816, the Sportsman's Hall parish came under O'Brien's care. As always, he pursued his ministry with zeal. His health began to fail, however, in the spring of 1820, and he retired to Mount St. Mary Seminary in Emmitsburg, Maryland. He was serving as chaplain to the Ursuline nuns at Port Tobacco, Maryland and in Baltimore when he died on November 1, 1823.

CHARLES BONAVENTURE MAGUIRE, O.F.M.

Despite the passage of the Bill of Rights, religious intolerance persisted in America. In Pittsburgh, however, attitudes toward Catholics changed noticeably during the tenure of Fr. O'Brien's successor.

Charles Bonaventure Maguire was born on December 16, 1770 near Dungannon in County Tyrone, Ireland. He prepared for the priesthood at the Catholic University of Louvain, Belgium. Erasmus wrote: "No one could graduate from Louvain without knowledge, manners and age."[23] Maguire was no exception. He was a tall, portly man with a commanding presence, a ruddy complexion and an appealing sense of humor. He was also an able linguist.

Fr. Maguire began his pastoral ministry in the Netherlands and Germany. He was in France during the Reign of Terror, 1793–1794. When his opposition to the revolutionaries became known, he was arrested. As the friar-priest was being led away, a local barrelmaker with whom he was friendly recognized him. The friend created a diversion that enabled Fr. Maguire to escape. For his courageous act, this gallant man was executed and became a martyr to the French Revolution.

Maguire fled France, and for the next six years, he taught theology at the College of St. Isidore in Rome. In 1815 the King of Bohemia commissioned Fr. Maguire to serve as chaplain to the diplomats at the court of Brussells. King Maximillian selected the Franciscan because of Maguire's linguistic abilities. At the end of the Battle of Waterloo, Fr. Maguire ministered to many of the wounded on the battlefield.

The instability of European governments so disturbed Fr. Maguire that he decided to become a missionary in America. After landing in Philadelphia in 1817, he was immediately assigned to the pastorate of Sportsman's Hall in western Pennsylvania. After a brief stop at Ebensburg, Fr. Maguire arrived at Holy Cross Church at Sportsman's Hall on November 27, 1817.

He was so pleased with the parishioners and the location that he promised to remain forever in that parish. Maguire was forced to break that promise in 1818, however, when Fr. O'Brien had to leave St. Patrick Church in Pittsburgh. Fr. Maguire succeeded O'Brien as pastor of Old St. Patrick's.

Fr. Thomas Heyden of Bedford wrote about Fr. Maguire's departure from Sportsman's Hall: "Moved by the wants of the Catholics in

Pittsburgh, he was transferred, or transferred himself thither, for there was no great order in those days — he made the Church in Pittsburgh what it is."[24]

Fr. Maguire's first entry in the parish registers of St. Patrick Church was on May 21, 1820.

Fr. Maguire was a zealous apostle. The sesquicentennial memorial of the University of Pittsburgh notes that as a man, friar, priest, scholar and citizen, Fr. Maguire was admired and respected by all who knew him.[25] The sterling example he set gave Catholics a greater measure of respectability in Pittsburgh. Well versed in the classics, Maguire was also knowledgeable about the political affairs of America and Europe. His rapier wit made him a favorite toastmaster at community affairs.

From 1822 to 1830, Fr. Maguire served as professor of modern languages at the Western University of Pennsylvania, now the University of Pittsburgh. By selecting him for this position, the city's educators indicated their high estimation of the Franciscan's academic credentials. He was the first Catholic priest to serve on the university's faculty.

As the population of Pittsburgh increased, the membership of St. Patrick parish continued to grow, and in 1822 Fr. Maguire had to double the size of the church.

Fr. Maguire had ambitions of founding a Franciscan friary, so he purchased 113 acres on the South Side of Pittsburgh in an area known as Sugar Tree Hill. His dream was not realized, though, because there were no other friars to form a fraternity.

Maguire's residence and parish office were on Liberty Avenue at Cherry Alley, across from the 10th Street intersection, about one block from St. Patrick Church, which was located near the intersection of Liberty Avenue and Grant Street at 11th Street. As membership in St. Patrick Parish continued to increase, a new church was built at 17th Street and Liberty Avenue. On March 21, 1935, this edifice was destroyed by fire. It was replaced by the present miniature structure at that location.

Fr. Demetrius Gallitzin, because of advancing age and physical impairment, retired from the office of vicar-general of western Pennsylvania. Maguire was appointed to succeed him on July 20, 1822. This appointment added extra duties to Maguire's long list of responsibilities; the vicar-general represented the Bishop of Philadelphia in supervising the churches in the western half of Pennsylvania.

Immigrants kept coming to Pittsburgh, and many of them found work building the Pennsylvania Canal which was begun in 1826. Many of the factories in Pittsburgh constantly needed laborers. Irish and other European newcomers increased the size of St. Patrick parish. Because of this increase, Fr. Patrick Rafferty was sent to St. Patrick's to assist with the parish ministry.

Five years after the church was enlarged, parishioners met on August 27, 1827 to discuss building a new church at a different location. Fr. Maguire's proposal was to locate the new church at Fifth Avenue and Grant Street; this suggestion was favorably received. This site was known as Grant's Hill because, at that location, Major James Grant's troops were defeated by French and Native American soldiers from Fort Duquesne on September 13, 1758.

Fr. Maguire desired to build a church that would be the greatest work of his life and ministry. The building was to be 175 feet by 76 feet, with a capacity of 2,500 persons. When these dimensions were made public, the *United States Catholic Miscellany*, the newspaper of the Diocese of Charleston, South Carolina, rebuked the Franciscan for anticipating a diocese in and for Pittsburgh.[26]

In 1828, Fr. Maguire arranged for the Sisters of St. Clare to establish a convent on the North Side of Pittsburgh. The location has since been known as Nunnery Hill. Dominican Fr. Vincent Raymacher was the sisters' chaplain and assisted Maguire in ministering to German immigrants. In 1830, Raymacher was succeeded by Fr. A. F. Van de Wejer, O.P., who fulfilled the same duties.

Bishops Conwell and Kenrick stopped in Pittsburgh on June 26, 1830 before continuing on to Philadelphia. The next day was Sunday, and Conwell administered confirmation at St. Patrick's.

By this time, the Catholic population in Pittsburgh was about 4,000. Acquiring money was always difficult, especially for the new St. Paul Church. On more than one occasion, work on the church had to be suspended until Fr. Maguire could obtain sufficient funds to continue the construction.

Maguire did not live to see his magnificent church completed. While caring for his parishioners, he became a victim of a cholera epidemic and died on July 17, 1833. He was buried on the property of St. Clare Convent, but when the convent was closed his remains were transferred to St. Mary Cemetery in Lawrenceville.

JOHN O'REILLY

Fr. John O'Reilly was born in Ireland on May 6, 1797. He emigrated to America and completed his seminary education and formation at Mount. St. Mary's in Emmitsburg, Maryland. He was ordained in Philadelphia by Bp. Conwell on March 10, 1827 and began his missionary work in eastern Pennsylvania. As the Pennsylvania Canal was built, he moved westward with it. In 1828, he was at Huntingdon County where he built a church which was dedicated by Bp. Conwell to the Most Holy Trinity on July 24, 1830.

Fr. O'Reilly also attended the Catholics at Bellefonte in Centre County, and at Newry in Blair County. In 1832, he came to Pittsburgh to assist Fr. Maguire at St. Patrick's while a new church was under construction. When Fr. Maguire died on July 17, 1833, O'Reilly became the pastor at St. Patrick's.[27]

Fr. O'Reilly lacked his predecessor's social graces, but he was a brilliant administrator. Within one year, he was able to complete construction of the church. It was dedicated on May 24, 1834 under the patronage of St. Paul by Bp. Kenrick. Fr. John Hughes, the future archbishop of New York, preached the sermon. With a capacity of 2,500 persons, St. Paul Church was one of the largest and finest churches in the United States.

Fr. Francis Masquelet, a linguist, came to St. Patrick's to assist O'Reilly in caring for German parishioners.

To gain their assistance in building the new church, Fr. Maguire had promised the Germans that the old church would be theirs. Fr. O'Reilly fulfilled this promise, but asked for an annual rent of $300 until the debt incurred in the construction of St. Paul Church was paid. The Germans accepted this offer, and Fr. Masquelet became their pastor at St. Patrick's.

At Fr. O'Reilly's request, three Sisters of Charity arrived in Pittsburgh on January 19, 1835 to take charge of St. Paul School. During that same year, the Sisters of St. Clare, who had founded the city's first convent in 1828, began leaving Pittsburgh. Many of these sisters returned to convents in Europe.

THE FACTORY CHURCH

Tensions began to develop in the German congregation. The annual rent for St. Patrick Church became a burden. Factions erupted when Fr. O'Reilly offered to sell the church to them for $6,000. One group favored the purchase of the church, but Fr. Masquelet and other parishioners were inclined to buy another site for their church. Masquelet's party prevailed, and they purchased a former cotton factory on Liberty Avenue at 14th Street. This location became known as The Factory Church. The second floor of this factory building was renovated as a worship site and dedicated under the title Saint Mary.[28]

On March 1, 1838, Fr. Henry Herzog succeeded Fr. Masquelet, but he stayed just seven months. Benedictine Fr. Nicholas Balleis ministered to the parishioners who remained at St. Patrick Church.

The initial life of the Factory Church was short lived. When Bp. Kenrick learned that the son of the former owner had opened a saloon on the first floor, he ordered that the church services be stopped. This enterprise evoked the following rhyme by an unknown poet:

> There's a spirit above; there's a spirit below.
> The Spirit above is the spirit of love,
> And the spirit below is the spirit of woe.
> The spirit above is the spirit divine,
> But the spirit below is the spirit of wine.

THE SISTERS OF CHARITY

The American Sisters of Charity were founded by St. Elizabeth Ann Seton. Elizabeth Ann Bayley was born in New York on August 28, 1774, two years before the Declaration of Independence was signed. She was baptized in the Episcopal Church. On January 25, 1794, she married William Magee Seton to whom she bore five children, two sons and three daughters.

William Seton was a businessman who had associations with the Filicchi brothers, who were merchants in Leghorn, Italy. Through business relations, they became close friends. Early in the 1800's, William Seton contracted tuberculosis and his health began to decline. In the hope that a change of climate might help him regain his health, and at the invitation of the Filicchi Brothers, the Seton family sailed to Italy. However, the journey and the change of climate were of little help, and William Seton died on December 27, 1803.

The grief-stricken young widow and her children were sheltered by the Filicchi family. During her stay with the Filicchis, Seton felt her first attraction toward Catholicism. Both Filicchi brothers and their wives were devout Catholics, and Seton was impressed with their way of life. She asked many questions about their faith. Antonio Filicchi advised her "to pray, to knock at the door."[29]

When the Seton family returned to New York, Elizabeth Ann Seton, in an attempt to support her children, opened a school for young children.

She continued to be drawn to the Catholic faith. The Filicchis had advised her to contact Bp. Carroll in Baltimore and Fr. Cheverus, the future bishop of Boston, for clarification of any question she might have. Both corresponded with her and instructed her. She made a profession of faith and was received into the Catholic Church on March 14, 1805 in St. Peter Church, Barclay Street, New York. She received the Sacrament of Confirmation on May 26, 1806 from Bp. Carroll.

Seton's embracing of Catholicism proved to be financially and socially disastrous. It caused some of her friends to ostracize her and to remove their children from her school. With the failure of the school, her financial problems continued to increase. At the invitation of Bp. Carroll, Seton and her children moved to Baltimore in June 1808. In September, she opened another school. Her dedication to children and her lifestyle attracted other young women to share in her work. With the donation of a farm near Emmitsburg, Maryland, Seton was able to move her school and her companions to this new site where they continued to live a communal life.

Encouraged by Bp. Carroll, Elizabeth Ann Seton pledged religious vows on March 25, 1809, and four months later, on July 31, 1809, with the reception of other members, the American Sisters of Charity were formed.

Bp. Carroll adapted the Rule of St. Vincent DePaul to meet American customs. This adaptation was approved and the Institute of

St. Elizabeth Ann Seton, the first native-born American saint, founded the American Sisters of Charity in 1809, an order that has been active in the Diocese of Pittsburgh since its early days.

the American Sisters of Charity was accepted by the Holy See. From Emmitsburg, the Sisters of Charity have developed into numerous branches whose members conduct schools, colleges, orphanages and hospitals in many locations.

Mother Seton died at Emmitsburg on January 4, 1821. She was beatified on March 17, 1963, and canonized on September 14, 1975. St. Elizabeth Ann Seton's feastday is observed on January 4.

THE REDEMPTORISTS

The Factory Church, as has already been noted, was a center of controversy. Happily, the conflicts it generated among German Catholics set the stage for the establishment of a new religious community in Pittsburgh.

The Congregation of the Most Holy Redeemer, or the Redemptorists, was experiencing difficulty in finding a place to establish an American house. Fortunately, Fr. Joseph Prost settled the Germans' problems. The patience and kindness demonstrated by this Redemptorist united the German immigrants in a harmonious parish within two weeks of his April 11, 1839 arrival in Pittsburgh. He asked the people to pray and to help him fulfill a vow that he had made while crossing the Atlantic Ocean in a dangerous storm. This vow was that the first church he would build would be dedicated to St. Philomena.

The Factory Church, which Bp. Kenrick had closed because of a saloon operating on the first floor, was again selected to be the place of worship for the German immigrants. The people cooperated in renovating the unfurbished church into an appropriate worship site.

With the bishop's permission, Fr. Prost blessed the building on November 1, 1839. The solemn dedication of the church by Bp. Kenrick took place on March 25, 1840. The former saloon was converted into school rooms.

Prost's superiors were disappointed because they thought he should have named the church in honor of St. Alphonsus Ligouri, founder of the Redemptorists. Ligouri had been canonized in 1839, the very year that Fr. Prost dedicated this Pittsburgh church to St. Philomena.

The number of German Catholics continued to grow. Soon, the renovated St. Philomena Church was inadequate. Plans were drawn for erecting a new church.

The cornerstone of the new church was laid on May 26, 1842, Corpus Christi day. Francis S. Shunk, a future governor of the state of Pennsylvania, attended the ceremonies. Two years later, when he ran for office, he was roundly criticized by local newspaper editors for fraternizing with Catholics.[30]

While serving as pastor of St. Philomena, Fr. Prost established the first permanent Redemptorist community in the western hemisphere. Once he settled in Pittsburgh, he was joined by five other Redemptorists.

ST. PHILOMENA CHURCH

The burden of completing and paying for St. Philomena Church fell to Fr. John Neumann, who had spent part of his novitiate in Pittsburgh. In 1844, he returned as pastor of St. Philomena Church and superior of the Redemptorist community.

To meet the increasing debts, Fr. Neumann organized a church building society. Each parishioner was asked to contribute five cents a week. Additional funds were borrowed, at a fixed rate of interest, from local Catholics. In his biography of Neumann, Fr. Michael J. Curley, C.SS.R., relates an anecdote:

> One incident of those building days shows the shrewdness of Neumann. A parishioner of St. Philomena's who had loaned a large sum of money to the Fathers suddenly became alarmed about his investment when rumors were circulated that it was not safe. Hurrying to the rectory, he demanded his money. The brother porter at the door hastened with the dread news to the almost bankrupt superior. A crisis it was indeed, for the news of failure to pay the loan promptly would have created a run on the rectory by others who had made loans, and this would have brought financial ruin. Neumann was equal to the occasion. With a bland smile he inquired of the creditor, "Do you wish your money in gold or silver?" "Oh, if that's the case," said the lender, "you can keep it, for it will be safe with you." And the depositor went away contented.[31]

Bp. O'Connor dedicated St. Philomena Church on October 4, 1846. It became the mother church of the many parishes dominated by German immigrants.

In the mid-1920s, St. Philomena's Church was transferred to Forward Avenue in Squirrel Hill. The school building was constructed first, and the church occupied one floor.

The Redemptorists, who came to Pittsburgh for the purpose of ministering to German Catholics, continued their work and were joined by two other religious congregations. In 1847, the School Sisters of Notre Dame arrived at St. Philomena's to teach girls. The Marianist Brothers came in 1860 and took charge of St. Philomena's school for boys.

Orphans from the parish were sent to St. Joseph Orphanage, established in 1851 on Troy Hill. Later, St. Joseph Orphanage accepted children from other German parishes throughout the Diocese. The orphanage functioned until 1938. North Catholic High School, on Troy Hill, presently occupies the site of the former St. Joseph Orphanage.

ST. JOHN NEUMANN

John Neumann, the third of six children, was born on March 28, 1811 at Prachaticz in Bohemia's Black Forest.

Neumann learned solid Christian principles from his devout Catholic parents. At age thirteen he entered the seminary at Budweis, the capital of the province situated at the confluence of the Malse and Vlatva rivers. In 1835 he completed his theology studies at the archepiscopal seminary connected with the University of Prague.

The local bishop postponed Neumann's ordination because he thought that he had sufficient priests for the needs of the Diocese.

When accounts of mission work in America reached Neumann, the young man applied for a post there and received a promise of acceptance in Philadelphia from an intermediary for that diocese. When he arrived in New York City on May 27, 1836, Neumann learned that the promise had been revoked. However, Bp. John Dubois, of New York, ordained Neumann on June 25, 1836 and assigned him to work in western New York state.

On July 12, 1836, Neumann arrived in Buffalo. For the next four years, he was an itinerant missionary. Neumann traveled on foot or horseback over rough, dusty roads ministering to Catholics. He was a firm believer in the axiom, "A house-going priest makes a church-going people."

St. John Neumann, a Redemptorist born in Bohemia, spent part of his novitiate in Pittsburgh and returned in 1844 as pastor of St. Philomena Church and superior of his religious community.

Fr. Neumann's energetic dedication to his strenuous duties affected his health. In 1840 he was obliged to rest at the Redemptorist House in Rochester, New York. While there, he resolved to join the congregation so that he might live in and with a community rather than endure a missioner's lonely existence.

With his bishop's permission, Neumann applied for and was admitted to the Redemptorists. Since the congregation did not have a fixed novitiate, Neumann — their first novice — was sent to the Redemptorist House in Pittsburgh.

A shortage of priests in Pittsburgh forced Neumann to combine his year of novitiate with pastoral ministry. In 14 months, the novice was in 12 religious houses. He was admitted to religious profession, as a Redemptorist, on January 16, 1842, and was the first Redemptorist to profess his vows in the United States. During the next two years, he worked in Baltimore and surrounding areas.

Fr. Neumann exhibited a gentle, peaceful manner and an ability to get along with people. These characteristics were tested over the next three years (1844–1847) when Neumann was pastor of Pittsburgh's St. Philomena Church. Despite his meager income, he managed to complete construction of a very large church.

His success in Pittsburgh earned Neumann an appointment as vice-regent and vice-provincial of the Redemptorists in America. And despite his protests to the contrary, Neumann became the fourth bishop of Philadelphia on March 28, 1852.

As bishop, Neumann was the same indefatigable man. He was a great promoter of the parochial school system, and he introduced the Forty House Devotion in the United States. In 1854, Neumann was among those present for the proclamation of the dogma of the Immaculate Conception.

While performing an act of charity for one of his pastors, Bp. Neumann collapsed and died on a Philadelphia sidewalk. The date was January 5, 1860. Bp. John Neumann was 49 years old.

Bp. Neumann was declared venerable by Pope Benedict XV on December 11, 1921. He was beatified on October 13, 1963, by Pope John XXIII, and canonized by Pope Paul VI on June 19, 1977. His feastday is January 5.[32]

EXPANSION

The number of Catholics in Pittsburgh increased, necessitating the building of more churches. In 1839 a portion of St. Paul Parish, at Grant and Fifth, was annexed to form St. Philip Parish in Crafton.

In October of 1840, Fr. Edward F. Garland was assigned to the pastorate of St. Patrick Church — the second English-speaking church in Pittsburgh.

Financial problems persisted for the Pittsburgh parishes, and diocesan expenses increased. So in 1839 — in an effort to obtain funds for the support of the Philadelphia seminary — Bp. Kenrick proposed that each parish pay *pew rental*. And, although the parishioners acknowledged their duty to support the seminary, this tax provoked strong opposition; it was viewed as an unwarranted use or misuse of clerical authority.

In June 1841, Fr. John O'Reilly resigned the pastorate of St. Paul Parish and went to Rome to join the Vincentians. His superiors, immediately recognizing O'Reilly's administrative abilities, assigned him to a succession of important duties and offices. Fr. O'Reilly died on March 4, 1862.

Fr. Michael O'Connor was named vicar-general for western Pennsylvania and also assumed the pastorate of St. Paul Church.

Fr. O'Connor's entry in his *Business and Letter Record* for June 17, 1841, notes that he: "Arrived in Pittsburgh on this day, (Thursday), lodging with Mrs. Timmons for $4 per week." This simple entry gave no indication of the turbulent times awaiting the new vicar-general, but the very next entry, for June 21 noted: "learned the difficulties of the German congregation."[33] This note referred to a dispute over the title to the property of the Factory Church. O'Connor made good use of his diplomatic skills and reached a compromise within two months. This was an example of the tactful skills and prudent methods that would mark O'Connor's tenure as vicar-general and bishop.

Fr. O'Connor dedicated St. Patrick Church, at Sugar Creek in Armstrong County, on July 29, 1841. The next year, on October 2, he dedicated the church of Sts. Simon and Jude in Blairsville, Indiana County. St. Patrick Church has been reconstructed in Sugar Creek.

Four

Michael J. O'Connor
1843–1860
First Bishop of Pittsburgh

The Diocese of Pittsburgh was founded on August 8, 1843 with the appointment of Father Michael O'Connor, pastor of St. Paul Church in Pittsburgh, as its first bishop.

Bishop Francis P. Kenrick's fatherly care laid the foundation of the Diocese of Pittsburgh. As administrator and diocesan Bishop of Philadelphia, he was very solicitous for the Catholic parishes in western Pennsylvania. His recommendation in 1835 that a diocese be established in Pittsburgh was not fulfilled until 1843, but during those years he guided the parishes of the future diocese.

FRANCIS KENRICK

Francis Patrick Kenrick was born on December 3, 1796, in Ireland. He prepared for the priesthood in Ireland and in Rome at the Pontifical Urban College of the Propaganda of the Faith, and was ordained in Rome on April 7, 1821. After ordination Kenrick was assigned to the Diocese of Bardstown, Kentucky.

In Bardstown, Fr. Kenrick was the rector of St. Joseph Seminary. He also taught theology, church history, liturgy, and Greek. In a short time he became an outstanding cleric in that missionary diocese.

In his role as his bishop's theologian, Fr. Kenrick accompanied Bp. Flaget to the First Provincial Council of Baltimore in 1829. In Baltimore he was selected to serve as the secretary of the Council. He performed these duties so well that the bishops were impressed with his efficiency. A recommendation that he be appointed to be the coadjutor bishop of Philadelphia and administrator of that diocese was forwarded to Rome. The Vatican approved the suggestion, and Fr. Kenrick was ordained by Bishop Flaget on June 6, 1830.

Bp. Kenrick's reception in Philadelphia was less than friendly, however. The Trustee Movement, which encouraged the laity to take over the temporal affairs of parishes, was strongly entrenched in that city. In 1827, Bp. Conwell had capitulated to the trustees by granting them a veto in pastoral appointments. Trusteeism had become the most significant internal conflict in American Catholicism, and it threatened ecclesiastical discipline in the United States.

The Trustees of the Philadelphia cathedral closed that building to Bp. Kenrick. The bishop placed the cathedral under interdict. The Trustees were inclined to ignore this censure. The bishop solved this impasse by an appeal to the parishioners. When he explained the Decrees of the First Provincial Council of Baltimore (1829), the people elected new trustees. They renounced any claim to nominate pastors, and they yielded all church property to episcopal control. Bp. Kenrick had control of this cathedral. The response of the people was so wholehearted that the recalcitrant trustees submitted to episcopal stewardship within three months.

The vastness of the Diocese of Philadelphia did not deter Bp. Kenrick from regular visits to the clergy, religious and laity scattered throughout the territory. The education of all committed to his care was also a concern. He fostered parochial schools, founded St. Charles Borromeo Seminary, and encouraged the establishment of Villanova and St. Joseph Universities.

Bp. Kenrick, together with Sisters of Charity, changed the attitude of many people toward Catholicism and endeared themselves to city residents by their solicitous care of the sick during a cholera epidemic.

On August 3, 1851, Bp. Kenrick was assigned to the Archdiocese of Baltimore. The next year he presided at the First Plenary Council of Baltimore. In the following year, 1853, he was deputed by the Vatican to ascertain the opinions of the American Bishops regarding the definition of the doctrine of the Immaculate Conception of the Blessed Virgin Mary.

Archbishop Kenrick proved to be a capable leader of the Catholic Church in the United States. When he died in Baltimore on July 8, 1863, he was 66. He had been a priest for 43 years and a bishop for 33 years.

MICHAEL J. O'CONNOR

Michael O'Connor, the first Bishop of Pittsburgh, was an outstanding prelate in the nineteenth century. Like his fellow clerics who guided the fortunes of American Catholicism at that time, O'Connor had to preach the gospel, supply workers for the missions and promote spiritual and material aid to his flocks.

American bishops fulfilled these duties under difficult circumstances because most of their parishioners were struggling farmers and poorly paid laborers. Bp. O'Connor, who met these obstacles with patience and courage, became one of the most brilliant lights in the American Catholic hierarchy.

Michael O'Connor was born near Cork, Ireland, September 17, 1810. He received his elementary education in O'Dowd Grammar School at Queenstown. As a youth, Michael exhibited a sharp mind and a solid respect for his faith. These qualities attracted the attention of Bp. William Coppinger of the Diocese of Cloyne and Ross, in County Cork, Ireland.

When Michael was only 14 years old, Bp. Coppinger sponsored the boy's education at schools in Paris and Rome, so he could pursue studies for the priesthood in the Pontifical Urban College of the Propagation of the Faith. O'Connor schoolmates in Rome were Francis Kenrick and Martin Spalding. Both became faithful and influential friends.

O'Connor finished his preparatory studies before he was old enough to be ordained. A dispensation was obtained and at age 23, Michael O'Connor was ordained on June 1, 1833, by Archbishop Gaetano Patrizi.

Bishop Michael J. O'Connor

Fr. O'Connor continued studies in Rome and earned a doctorate in theology in 1834. Cardinal Nicholas Wiseman, rector of the English College in Rome, participated at Fr. O'Connor's public defense of his doctoral dissertation and was impressed by the young priest's brilliant mind.

Pope Gregory XVI also recognized O'Connor's talents and the two men solidified a personal friendship. When O'Connor knelt at his feet, the pope twisted his handkerchief around O'Connor's forehead, saying: "If it were a crown of gold, you would deserve it."[1]

While in Rome, Fr. O'Connor taught sacred scripture at the Pontifical Urban College of the Propagation of the Faith. He also served as vice-rector of the Irish College, and at times, as an intermediary between Irish and American bishops in their correspondence with the Vatican.

The English-speaking bishops found it a great advantage to have O'Connor edit their petitions or proposals and represent them to the proper office. O'Connor's ability as an interpreter and translator earned him the designation, "The Pope's Linguist."[2]

In 1835, Bp. Bartholomew Crotty of the Diocese of Cloyne and Ross recalled O'Connor to Ireland to join the faculty of a planned diocesan seminary. O'Connor was assigned as a temporary curate in the parish of Fermoy, and later as chaplain at Presentation Convent in Doneraile.

The proposed diocesan seminary did not materialize. O'Connor was a teacher at heart and desired a more active ministry. He considered applying for a professorship at Maynooth Seminary in Dublin.

Before this proposal was accepted, another opportunity was presented by Fr. Peter Kenrick, who was visiting Ireland. Peter Kenrick was the brother of the coadjutor bishop of Philadelphia, Francis Kenrick.

Fr. Kenrick convinced Fr. O'Connor that he could fulfill, in the Diocese of Philadelphia, his desire to be a missionary priest and a teacher. Accompanied by his 16-year-old brother, James, Fr. Michael O'Connor arrived in Philadelphia on November 10, 1838. He was immediately placed in charge of St. Charles Boromeo Seminary. He also labored in the mission parish at Norristown and erected the

Church of St. Francis Xavier at Fremont.

O'Connor's erudition and proficiency so impressed Kenrick that at the Fourth Provincial Council of Baltimore in 1840, Kenrick recommended O'Connor for the episcopacy.

To groom his protege, Bp. Kenrick chose O'Connor to accompany him on his 1840 visit of the Diocese of Philadelphia, which at that time encompassed Pennsylvania, Delaware and part of New Jersey. From July to September they visited the parishes in western Pennsylvania.[3]

One year later, on June 17, 1841, O'Connor was appointed pastor of St. Paul Church in Pittsburgh and vicar-general for western Pennsylvania. Problems awaited the new leader. On June 21, O'Connor wrote that he had "learned the difficulties of the German congregations."

A dispute with the former pastor of St. Paul Church regarding the payment of rent for St. Patrick Church had caused friction within the German congregation. This financial problem was minor compared to O'Connor's tense relations with German personnel in the Diocese.

The strongest financial supporters of the American missions were the Leopoldine Association, under the supervision of King Ludwig of Bavaria and the Pontifical Society of Lyon, France. These charitable organizations dispersed their funds to the bishops, or to some individual clerics who met the qualifications for their grants.

Since Germany was the principal source of financial assistance, the pastors of the German parishes felt that they should be the recipients of the entire donations. The vicar-general considered that the monetary aid was to be used throughout the territory. These divergent views were a discordant note between the clergy and their superiors which rang for many years.

O'Connor was immersed in his pastoral and administrative duties. However, he retained a fervent wish to be a teacher and join the Jesuits. But O'Connor knew that he would need the pope's permission to make any changes. He was propelled into action when John England, the illustrious bishop of Charleston, South Carolina, died on April 11, 1842. O'Connor was the preferred appointee to be England's successor.

A delay in naming a bishop for Charleston, and the firm conviction of the bishops of the province that there should be a diocese in Pittsburgh, placed O'Connor as the leading candidate for the new diocese. But he opposed either plan.

While the American bishops gathered for the Fifth Provincial Council in Baltimore, in May, 1843, Michael O'Connor tried to circumvent his appointment as bishop by traveling to Rome. He planned to ask the pope for permission to become a Jesuit.

But the decrees of the Fifth Provincial Council reached the pope's hands before O'Connor saw him. As he knelt at Pope Gregory's feet, the pope remarked: "You shall be a bishop first, and a Jesuit afterwards. I will not let you rise from your knees until you promise to accept the Diocese of Pittsburgh."[4]

The documents for the erection of the new diocese and the appointment of Bp. O'Connor were signed on August 8, 1843. Michael O'Connor was ordained bishop on August 15, 1843 by Cardinal Fransoni in the chapel of the Irish College in Rome.

O'Connor knew the people in Pittsburgh were poor. Before returning to America, he visited mission-minded organizations in Europe: the Leopoldine Society of Vienna, Austria, and the Society for the Propagation of the Faith in Lyon and Paris. During each visit, he requested financial support for his diocese.

O'Connor realized the great need for priests and nuns. He traveled to his native Ireland, visiting Maynooth Seminary in Dublin and St. Leo Convent in Carlow. At Maynooth, twenty seminarians responded to his appeal. He told the faculty and students that in Pittsburgh they would have "plenty of labor and little for it."[5] Because of the scarcity of funds, his selection was limited to eight advanced seminarians.

At St. Leo Convent, the bishop persuaded the superior of the newly-founded Sisters of Mercy to send volunteers to establish a religious community in Pittsburgh. Seven sisters were chosen from 23 volunteers. Sister Francis Xavier Warde, R.S.M., was the superior of the first group of nuns to come to the United States.

In hopes that he could quickly establish a seminary in Pittsburgh, Bp. O'Connor brought Fr. Richard Wilson from the Irish College in Rome to Pittsburgh. The shortage of funds set the limit of the number of volunteers that the bishop could bring with him.[6]

After a 30-day voyage across the Atlantic, they landed in New York on December 13, 1843. Following short visits in New York and Philadelphia, they arrived in Pittsburgh on December 20. Wilson and the seminarians resided at the bishop's house. The Sisters of Mercy were hosted by the Sisters of Charity for two days. On December 22, they moved into a 12-room house at 800 Penn Street, now Penn Avenue.

On Christmas Day in St. Paul Cathedral, Bp. O'Connor explained the nature of his responsibilities and promised to fulfill them. The same promise was conveyed to the priests and people of the Diocese by a pastoral letter.

During his tenure as pastor of St. Paul Church in Pittsburgh, O'Connor learned how to organize and guide a diocese. The priests were pleased with his leadership. Fr. Thomas Heyden expressed their acceptance in a letter to Fr. James Ambrose Stillinger: "We certainly got a bishop in whom we shall be delighted."[7]

Immediately after his arrival, Bp. O'Connor began many projects. He conducted a diocesan synod for priests and founded a seminary. He established a diocesan newspaper and began building a rectory for the cathedral. He also opened the Chapel of the Nativity, "for the use of the Colored Catholics of the city."[8]

On February 4, 1844, Bp. O'Connor ordained Fr. Thomas McCullagh, one of the seminarians who accompanied him from Ireland. This was the bishop's first ordination in the Diocese. The next month, on March 3, O'Connor ordained four more priests: John Brady, Thomas O'Flaherty and Michael Mitchell from Ireland, and Robert Kleinendam from Germany. On September 1, 1844, he ordained Tobias Mullen, Peter Brown, and Patrick Duffy.

In the spring of the following year, a fire destroyed the homes of many parishioners on April 10, 1845. The fire started at Second Avenue (Boulevard of the Allies) and Ferry Street (Stanwix) and burned out everything from Fourth Avenue to the Monongahela River, as far as the present Tenth Street bridge. Bp. O'Connor and many Catholics assisted the families who were left homeless.

WOMEN RELIGIOUS

In the nineteenth century, the superiors of religious women exercised more managerial responsibility than any other women in American society. They directed their own organizations as well as educational and charitable institutions. They also supervised the missionary activities of their members.

Bp. O'Connor's experience with groups of religious women was not always pleasant. When he returned to Pittsburgh as bishop, O'Connor brought with him seven Sisters of Mercy from Carlow, Ireland. The nuns eventually helped O'Connor to achieve many of his goals for the Diocese in their works of education and charity.

Before the Diocese was established, there were only two religious communities in Pittsburgh: the Sisters of Charity and the Redemptorists. The Sisters of Charity operated the St. Paul schools, the orphanage and an academy for girls. The Redemptorists, whose primary mission was service to German Catholics, had extended their ministries by establishing missions outside the city in Glenshaw and McKeesport.

O'Connor served as moderator to the Sisters of Mercy. His favoritism toward this religious community provoked the withdrawal of the Sisters of Charity from the Diocese in the summer of 1845. It also was the basis for complaints of discrimination by the Sisters of Notre Dame.

When Bp. O'Connor granted approval for the Sisters of Mercy to operate a second tuition academy for girls, the Sisters of Charity foresaw a sharp decline of their very necessary income. The tuition payments to their academy were the main support for the sisters and their institutions. Anticipating financial difficulties, the Council at their Motherhouse at Emmitsburg, Maryland, transferred the Sisters of Charity from Pittsburgh to fields of labor in other dioceses.[9]

The Sisters of Notre Dame were brought to the Diocese of Pittsburgh under the auspices of the Redemptorists. They did not seek the permission and consent of Bp. O'Connor. At first the sisters resided in a convent at St. Mary's, Pennsylvania. Their failure to follow church rules caused O'Connor to delay his approval of the Sisters of Notre Dame until he could investigate the community and its rule.

O'Connor allowed the Sisters of Notre Dame to remain at St.

A page from his 1846 "business and letter record" describes Bishop O'Connor's August travels to Beaver and New Bedford.

Mary's. But his delay in granting permission accounts for the fact that the motherhouse of the Sisters of Notre Dame is in Baltimore, Maryland, instead of Pittsburgh.

In letters to their financial supporters in Europe, the Sisters of Notre Dame frequently complained that the "Irish Bishop" granted preferential treatment to the Sisters of Mercy, "the nuns he brought over from Ireland."[10]

THE SISTERS OF MERCY

Catherine McAuley was born in Dublin, Ireland, in 1778. Her father was a wealthy businessman who had a deep regard for the welfare of others. Although he died when she was only five years old, Catherine remembered his good example. The fatherless girl experienced difficulties in a foster home, in poverty and from religious persecution.

In her early forties, McAuley received her inheritance. Motivated by personal experience and her father's example, she began to devote all her energy to helping the poor.

On September 24, 1827, Catherine McAuley opened Our Lady of Mercy Home as a shelter for working-class women in Dublin. The example of her charity attracted other women to assist her. Living in community, Catherine and her companions entered into a prayerful, disciplined life. Their works of charity and their community living became a topic of gossip in Dublin. Some of the chatter was in admiration, some was malicious.

The bishop of Dublin, Daniel Murray, challenged Catherine McAuley and her associates to either form a religious community or disband. To learn the fundamentals of forming a religious order, Catherine and two other women went, in 1830, to a novitiate of the Presentation Order in Dublin.

On December 12, 1831 the three women pronounced their vows. Their profession of vows of poverty, chastity and obedience served as the foundation of the Sisters of Mercy. In the early nineteenth century, religious women usually lived within a convent. But a cloistered life would limit the goals and work of the new order. Their mission was to seek out the poor.

Mother Catherine McAuley founded the Sisters of Mercy, who were brought to the Diocese of Pittsburgh by Bishop O'Connor in 1843.

While he was in Rome as a student and as a young priest, Michael O'Connor was a liaison between English-speaking bishops and the Vatican. Familiar with the Vatican, he was able to gain approval for this new type of religious order, which would permit its members to help the poor. They became known as the "Walking Nuns" by the people of Dublin.

Before her death in 1841, Mother Catherine McAuley's religious daughters numbered more than 100 members in 14 convents in Ireland and England. In 1841, Pope Gregory XVI gave final approval to the rule of the Sisters of Mercy.

GERMANIC CONTROVERSIES

One of O'Connor's first problems was a dispute with European societies that gave financial support to American missions. The most generous supporters were the Leopoldine Association, under the supervision of King Ludwig of Bavaria, and the Pontifical Society of Lyon, France. These charitable organizations dispensed their funds to bishops, or sometimes to individual clerics who met their qualifications for grants.

One of the qualifications was that the money be spent to educate and assist German immigrants. But some American bishops used the money for general expenses. This caused German priests in America to accuse bishops of neglecting German parishes in their dioceses.

Responding to these accusations, the Leopoldine Association, in 1843, asked American bishops to submit detailed accountings of how the grants were spent. The request incensed American bishops, who insisted that, "all have been conscientious in expending the money granted to them."[11]

O'Connor rejected the complaints of German priests. He contended that the European societies gave more credence to these objections by individual priests than to the bishops' reports, and made their grants on ethnic preferences.

In 1845, the Leopoldine Association gave 8,000 gulden, or about $4,000, to German parishes in the Diocese of Pittsburgh. By contrast, in the same year, O'Connor received 1,680 gulden, or about $760, and was told that further assistance would not be awarded because he was not considered "friendly to the Germans."[12]

But O'Connor's biggest difficulty with German Catholics came in his dealings with Fr. Boniface Wimmer, superior of the Benedictines and founder of St. Vincent Abbey and Seminary.

Sebastian Wimmer was ordained a priest of the Diocese of Regensburg, Bavaria, in 1831. At that time, King Ludwig I of Bavaria was fostering a revival of Catholicism in his country. The faith had almost been destroyed under Emperor Napoleon. To achieve his goal, King Ludwig called for the restoration of the Benedictine Abbey of Metten, in the Diocese of Regensburg. To assist in this restoration, Sebastian Wimmer transferred to the Benedictine Order in 1832, and accepted the name "Boniface" because of his deep admiration of the original Apostle to the Germans — St. Boniface.

Ten years later, Fr. Boniface Wimmer recognized the extensive migration of European people to the United States and became concerned about the spiritual care of German immigrants. He expressed a desire to go to the United States and establish a Benedictine monastery. His superiors did not approve his suggestion. Boniface appealed to King Ludwig, who also rejected the proposal.

For the next three years, his plans met with objections. Finally, on November 8, 1845, he published an anonymous article entitled "Uber die missionem" in the newspaper *Augsburger Postzeitung.*

In this article, Boniface claimed that the conversion of most of the countries of Europe was exclusively the work of Benedictines, and that the Benedictine Order was, "the most competent to relieve the great want of priests in America."[13]

King Ludwig, who had a great love for the Benedictines, was impressed by the article. When he learned that the author was Boniface Wimmer, the King changed his mind about Wimmer's proposal. He sent for him and gave financial support to this endeavor.

When Fr. Boniface published this article, Peter Henry Lemcke was visiting his native Germany. Lemcke, who left the Lutheran Church to become a Catholic priest, was pastor of Carrolltown in the Diocese of Pittsburgh. He had approval from O'Connor to solicit German clerics to come to the Diocese because the bishop had "an immediate need for additional German priests."[14]

As part of his search, Lemcke visited the Abbey of Metten. He consulted with Fr. Boniface and invited him to come to Pennsylvania. Lemcke offered his own farm at Carrolltown as an idyllic location for a German monastery. His offer was accepted.

When Boniface arrived at Carrolltown, Cambria County, with eighteen prospective Benedictines, he was disappointed. The land was hilly and unsuitable for establishing a farming community of religious men.

Fr. Boniface visited O'Connor and expressed his dissatisfaction. The bishop welcomed him and his men to the Diocese. He also gave the Benedictines the chance to move to St. Vincent Church in Westmoreland County. When Boniface accompanied Bp. O'Connor to the proffered location and saw the gently rolling hills, he accepted the bishop's offer.

O'Connor was delighted with the prospect of having a monastery and a seminary within the Diocese. But what should have been an ideal undertaking became a source of prolonged tension throughout the remainder of his tenure in Pittsburgh. These two determined clergymen knew what they wished to achieve but their approaches differed.

Difficulties regarding title to the property at St. Vincent began almost immediately. Fr. Boniface demanded a clear title to the property. O'Connor was willing to grant the title on the condition that diocesan students could be admitted to the proposed seminary on the same terms as German students and that a diocesan priest be appointed as an instructor and prefect to maintain an American influence in the school.

Boniface refused to accept these conditions. He supported his refusal on the basis that he was a Benedictine who was to establish a Benedictine Monastery, that he had come to America to establish a German seminary and that his base of support was German money.

Fr. Boniface's plan was to establish a Catholic center, around which small German communities would form. With this foundation, German Catholics would be able to worship God and receive a Catholic education. The school would extend through all levels, including the seminary which would provide for the urgent need of German priests.

Boniface resented the proposition that students at St. Vincent's would learn to speak English. He worried that they would be cast into a mold fashioned to meet the needs of American Catholics. He also objected to teaching English because he thought that German immigrants who learned the English language would lose their faith.

O'Connor was disappointed that the new Benedictine monastery and seminary would not offer him any assistance. He needed priests willing to work in the missions and of the 19 people at St. Vincent's at that time, Boniface was the only priest. Moreover, Fr. Boniface's plan for the seminary, excluding diocesan students, eliminated any benefit of additional diocesan priests.

Because of the prevalence of anti-Catholic prejudice, the bishop was concerned that what appeared as an emphasis on German nationalism would be an added support to the claims of the "Nativists" that anti-Americanism prevailed in the Catholic Church.

In 1848, the matter was resolved. Boniface received title and permanent possession of the property. He was appointed pastor of St. Vincent and gained canonical status for his Benedictine foundation. In return, diocesan students were admitted to the seminary.

The next problem that arose was most unusual. The chief source of funds for Fr. Boniface was the Leopoldine Association. In 1849, a nephew of Boniface who was migrating to the United States was entrusted with funds for his uncle. The nephew squandered most of the money on himself. In an attempt to obtain money for restitution, the nephew urged Boniface to purchase a brewery and tavern in Indiana, Pennsylvania, about thirty miles from the monastery. Fr. Boniface made the purchase and had the deed recorded in his own name.

The nephew mismanaged the brewery and it failed. To recoup this loss, Benedictine brothers who were expert at brewing beer were sent by Wimmer to Indiana and put in charge of the brewery. The operation became successful. The brewery and tavern made and sold beer at wholesale and retail prices.

When O'Connor learned of this venture, he quickly ordered that the tavern be sold, rented or closed. Boniface, anxious to recover the investment, delayed any action on the bishop's order.[15]

Around this time, Bp. O'Connor received from Rome the document of official elevation of St. Vincent Monastery to the status of an abbey. O'Connor refused to execute the document until the tavern controversy was settled.

O'Connor's position regarding the operation of the tavern and the elevation of St. Vincent's to an Abbey is often badly distorted in biographies of Fr. Boniface. The bishop's delay in fulfilling that order as well as elevating Boniface to the status of abbot has been blamed on O'Connor's dedication to the Total Abstinence Movement. It also has been claimed that the bishop opposed the drinking of beer by the monks. The bishop's real objection was not to the consumption of beer, but that the monastery owned and operated a public tavern.

Fr. Boniface was most anxious to receive the promotion, which he had requested. To hasten an official decision, he went to Rome. There, he presented his view of the situation to King Ludwig. On past occasions, the monarch had used his political clout on behalf of Boniface with Benedictine superiors and ecclesiastical authorities in Rome.

O'Connor was disturbed by Boniface's attempt to bypass his official position by resorting to links with European royalty and their secular influence.

The intervention by King Ludwig, and his agent, Ambassador Graf von Spaur, was unsuccessful. Out of deference to Bp. O'Connor, the Sacred Congregation for the Propagation of the Faith withheld decisive action until the bishop could explain his reasons for delaying the execution of Rome's orders.

Eventually, O'Connor's explanation was upheld by the Vatican. When the brewery and tavern in Indiana were closed, the order to elevate St. Vincent to the status of an abbey was carried out.

The insinuation that Bp. O'Connor was ruthless in his treatment of the Germans in the Diocese of Pittsburgh was unfounded. The bishop was always concerned for their spiritual welfare and frequently bemoaned the scarcity of German priests. Despite his disagreements with Fr. Boniface, Bp. O'Connor always retained a great respect for him and for the Benedictine Community.

THE PASSIONISTS

In July 1852, Bp. O'Connor went to Rome as a delegate of the First Plenary Council of Baltimore. He presented the results of the council's deliberations and discussions to Pius IX.

While in Rome, O'Connor resided at the Irish College, which was close to the Passionists' headquarters. He visited the major superior, Fr. Anthony Testa, C.P., and asked him to establish a Passionist monastery in the Diocese of Pittsburgh. Undaunted by an initial refusal, O'Connor pursued his petition and Fr. Anthony consented to send three priests and one brother to Pittsburgh.

The missionaries accompanied O'Connor during his visit with Pius IX, who gave his blessing for the Passionists' new venture. Short of funds and unsuccessful in appeals to the Society for the Propagation of the Faith, O'Connor did manage to bring the four missionaries to America with him.

After landing in Philadelphia on November 15, 1852, the Passionists were housed at St. Charles Seminary. Fr. Anthony Calandri, C.P., the superior of the group, accompanied O'Connor to Baltimore, where he reported to Abp. Kenrick on the result of his visit with the pope.

While the bishop and superior were in Baltimore, Stanislaus Parcyzk, C.P., who was fluent in German, was welcomed by Bp. John Neumann of Philadelphia. He assisted Neumann with two annoying problems. One was a young Polish youth who had been condemned to death for a crime which later events proved he did not perform. Protesting his innocence, the youth began to blaspheme, and refused to be reconciled. Fr. Stanislaus was able to move this unfortunate youth to be reconciled before his execution. The other was a parish church which because of trusteeism was under interdict and refused the overtures of Bp. Neumann. In the short time that he had, Fr. Stanislaus convinced the parishioners to be reconciled with their bishop. Fr. Albinus Magno, C.P., and Br. Lawrence di Giacomo, C.P., used the time to begin studying English. Their sojourn in Philadelphia was valuable to all.[16]

The Passionists who arrived in Pittsburgh on November 22, 1852, lived temporarily at the bishop's house on Grant Street until a location for a permanent monastery could be found.

O'Connor offered two possible locations to Calandri. One site adjoined St. Mary Cemetery in Lawrenceville. The other was in Birmingham, on the South Side of the city, near the seminary, the orphanage, and the church for Germans. The Lawrenceville location was chosen. But before construction began, Fr. Anthony changed his mind and selected the land on the South Side of the Monongahela River, which was on top of a hill overlooking Birmingham.

The parishioners of St. Michael Church offered to support the church and the monastery which were to be built in their neighborhood. The motivation for this support was that Fr. Stanislaus would serve as the pastor of St. Michael's.[17]

The Passionists were officially admitted to the Diocese on May 27, 1853. Frs. Anthony and Albinus could not have been more different. Fr. Anthony was a serious, inflexible man. As a superior, he was timid and indecisive except when a question of observing the rules of his community arose.

Fr. Anthony's rigid training did not allow for any alteration in the life of a religious. Fr. Albinus, although strong-willed and assertive, was better at adapting to the American way of life. Sometimes there was discord but it did not disrupt the community.

Though ineffective as an administrator, Fr. Anthony was an excellent preacher of parish missions. His English was imperfect but his zeal and sincerity conveyed his message. The Passionists proved their valor and won the hearts of Catholics and other citizens in the city who witnessed their attention to the sick during an 1854 cholera epidemic. About 250 persons died during the epidemic.

The first observance of the feast of Paul of the Cross, founder of the Passionists, was on April 30, 1854, in the Passionists' unfinished chapel. The new monastery was blessed by Bp. O'Connor on June 4, 1854.

As the community grew, Fr. Calandri willingly relinquished the office of superior. On July 22, 1854, he was succeeded by John Dominic Tarlattini, C.P., an excellent administrator who is recognized as the founder of the Passionists in America.[18]

Parishes which were formed from St. Paul Monastery were St. Ann's in Castle Shannon, St. Joseph's in Mount Oliver and St. Martin's in the West End.

ANTI-CATHOLIC PREJUDICE

Anti-Catholic prejudice has always been a challenge to the faithful. John Higham of Johns Hopkins University wrote in the 1980s: "The most luxuriant, tenacious traditions of paranoic agitation in America, has been anti-Catholicism."[19] The Harvard historian, Arthur Schlesinger, Sr., has written that Catholic bashing is "the deepest bias in the history of the American people."[20] Fr. Demetrius Gallitzin, the Apostle of the Alleghenies, complained in the nineteenth century about the "violent attacks, unjust prejudice, and foul calumnies against the Catholic Church."[21]

The Nativists, so called because they believed that American democracy and Roman Catholicism were incompatible, considered Catholicism a threat to the freedom of American political institutions and to Protestant morals.

After 1815, waves of European immigrants, especially those from Germany and Ireland, transformed a small minority of Catholics into the single largest religious denomination in America. Commerce and industry continued to attract new settlers.

Between 1840 and 1850, the population of Allegheny County doubled in size from approximately 70,000 to 138,200. The Catholic growth and expansion had awakened Protestant fear of popery.

The Nativists felt threatened because they were outnumbered, and they feared that their employment opportunities were endangered. In their crusade to keep America Protestant, the Nativists foisted a wave of anti-Catholic propaganda upon the American public. The dominance of the prominent Scotch-Irish settlers can account for the bitterness of the anti-Catholic prejudice.

The Order of Orange continued in America the anti-Catholic bigotry that was practiced in northern Ireland. Since the Scotch-Irish were early settlers in Pittsburgh they had attained political offices in the fledgling city. Most newspapers were denominational organs and strongly anti-Catholic. In April 1844, the *Presbyterian Advocate* printed a warning for non-Catholics: "the devil and the Roman Catholics will take their territory from them."[22]

Though primarily an outgrowth of the Order of United Americans,

The original Mercy Hospital, the first hospital in western Pennsylvania, was founded by the Sisters of Mercy in 1846.

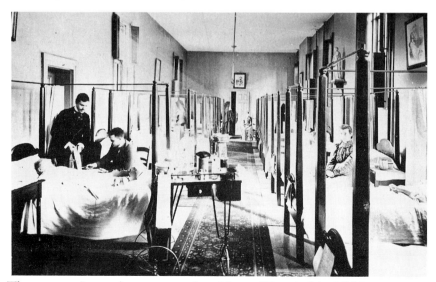

The women's ward was opened at Mercy Hospital in 1848.

a secret society whose members' responses to questions about the Order and its purposes was, "I don't know," the "Know-Nothing" movement was an amalgam of secret societies and militant Protestants that eventually became a political party — The American Party.

The establishment of the Diocese of Pittsburgh in 1843 with Bp. O'Connor residing in the city was an event which fumed Protestant fears and anti-Catholic activities. One of O'Connor's first directives was the establishment of a chapel for African-American Catholics. There was immediate reaction. The pastor of the Chapel of the Nativity, Fr. Richard Wilson, was accused of being pro-slavery by some of the local clergy. It was also alleged that the chapel was just a place to assemble African-Americans and sell them into slavery. These accusations by Protestant ministers made the African-American Catholics fearful, and the chapel at the corner of Smithfield Street and Diamond Street (Forbes Avenue) was abandoned.

In 1844, anti-Catholic violence erupted in Philadelphia. In November of that year, after learning of threats against Catholic buildings, Pittsburgh Catholics became defensive. Bp. O'Connor told his parishioners, "Stir neither hand or foot, but if they attempt to fire your asylum or your church, I will head you."[23] The bishop's promise to lead any necessary defense averted the threatened activity. Even charitable institutions did not escape vilification.

When Mercy Hospital, the first hospital in western Pennsylvania, was founded in 1846, it was severely criticized by the *Presbyterian Advocate*. The newspaper continued its attacks on the hospital for several years. On April 22, 1848, Mrs. Jane Gray Swisshelm, a Protestant and editor of the *Sunday Visitor* described one article in the *Presbyterian Advocate* as "a mean, ungentlemanly, unchristian and brutal attack" on the Sisters of Mercy. She further commented that the article was "the filthiest one I have ever seen."[24]

In 1850, the Protestant Association of Pittsburgh and Allegheny County made plans to burn Mercy Hospital and other Catholic buildings. Luckily, a member of this secret society revealed the plans. Bp. O'Connor ordered that all Catholic buildings be guarded day and night. As a result, no vandalism occurred.

Joe Barker was the most virulent foe of Catholics in Pittsburgh.

Between 1845 and 1850, this ignorant, bigoted man preached tirades in the streets against Bp. Michael O'Connor and his followers, whom he called "Mickies."

Barker did not allow anything Catholic to escape his vituperation. He was arrested, tried and found guilty of drunken harangues against Catholics. While Barker was still in prison, the voters elected him mayor of Pittsburgh in 1850. Because he had been elected to that office, Gov. William Johnston ordered Barker released from prison.

Mayor Barker exercised his power in short order. He had O'Connor arrested on a trumped-up charge of creating a plumbing nuisance at Mercy Hospital. In the absence of any official justice (because court was not in session during the month of August), the mayor presided at the bishop's trial and found him guilty. To avoid the farce of further litigation, the bishop paid the fine of $20, under protest.

Joe Barker's attacks against Catholics occasioned Judge Benjamin Patton of the Court of Common Sessions to remark: "The forbearance and patience the (Catholics) have shown during that long range of outrages, injustice and oppression, reflect great credit on them and the faith they profess."[25]

Mayor Barker's term was limited to one year. However, he continued his harangues against Catholics until his tragic death in 1862, when in an inebriated condition, after one of his sermons, he was struck by a train in the Manchester district of the city.

At the same time, religious prejudice was prevalent in the newspapers. The *Gazette* and the *Presbyterian Advocate* were the most vociferous in their attacks against Catholics. Promotion of Nativism was apparently their goal. On September 27, 1844, the *Gazette* stated as its position: "The great question reaching the hearts, and moving the mass of people is . . . Whether our Commonwealth is to regain its Protestant Character."[26]

In 1851, in a second attempt to level the streets at Grant's Hill, city workers graded the area and lowered Fifth Avenue and Grant Street ten feet. This excavation left St. Paul Cathedral isolated on a 20-foot stump of dirt, and the foundations of the church were damaged. A flight of steps had to be constructed for access to the church. That same year, on May 6, the Cathedral was destroyed by a fire of questionable

The original St. Paul Cathedral was destroyed by fire in 1851. This picture shows how the cathedral was left on a hill of dirt 20 feet above street level when Fifth Avenue and Grant Street were leveled.

origin. The stump of dirt had to be leveled and a second St. Paul Cathedral was built on the same site. This edifice, facing Grant Street, was consecrated on June 24, 1855. The Union Trust Building now occupies this location.

The industrial development of Pittsburgh continued to attract newcomers. Many of these were immigrants from Catholic countries in Europe. This influx of Catholics was perceived as an ominous sign by the Know-Nothings. Almost every year, some event occurred to arouse anti-Catholic prejudice.

Two visitors to Pittsburgh fueled outbursts of hostility toward the Catholic church and its members.

In 1852, Louis Kossuth, leader of Hungary's ill-fated attempt to obtain independence from Austria, came to Pittsburgh for an eight-day visit. He was welcomed as a symbol of liberty. At triumphant receptions he was also proposed as a symbol of Protestantism. His talks aroused anti-Catholic sentiments and renewed Nativist bigotry. But as the week progressed, his constant anti-Catholic speeches became monotonous and his popularity waned.

A year later, tensions increased when Abp. Gaetano Bedini, was asked by Pius IX to visit the Unites States and deliver a letter to President Franklin Pierce. The purpose of Bedini's visit was to determine the suitability of sending a nuncio, or some other papal representative, to the United States. He was also commissioned to visit some dioceses in an endeavor to restore peace to parishes troubled by trusteeism.

Bedini was a veteran diplomat and fluent in five languages: Latin, English, German, French and Italian. He was frequently selected to perform many difficult tasks. He had been assigned to Bologna at the time the Austrian government executed a number of Italian rebels. Even though Abp. Bedini did not have previous knowledge of these executions, he was caricatured by an apostate priest, Fr. Gavazzi, as *The Bloody Butcher of Bologna*. Because of these accusations, wherever Bedini visited, he was classified as an agent of Vatican inquisition and as a symbol of foreign intervention in United States affairs.

Bedini could not have arrived at a less propitious time. He became a convenient target for anti-Catholic bigotry. Anti-clerical Italian exiles had an opportunity to revile the church. These radical Italians sought cooperation from their counterparts among the Germans and fomented the fury of the Nativists.

When Bedini arrived for a five-day visit in Pittsburgh, Bp. O'Connor had been transferred to the Diocese of Erie. But O'Connor came from Erie to accompany Bedini on his tour of western Pennsylvania between December 10 and 15 of 1853.

On Sunday, December 11, at the conclusion of a service at St. Patrick Church, the bishops were accosted by a crowd of ruffians. Bedini did not recognize the danger and peace was preserved by the forbearance and prudence of Bp. O'Connor.

While Bedini was in Pittsburgh, Mayor Robert Riddle was pressured by anti-Catholics to prevent any public meetings with the archbishop.

Bp. O'Connor appealed to the mayor and defended the right of Catholics to have public demonstrations. He emphasized the rights of citizens to assemble and argued that such gatherings did not violate any laws. Mayor Riddle had to agree that he had no reason to interfere with these meetings. Many non-Catholics were embarrassed by activities of the Nativists and they protested the outrageous treatment Bedini received while in Pittsburgh. When the archbishop quietly left Pittsburgh on December 15, protests against him and the Church subsided.[27]

The constancy and the extent of anti-Catholic bigotry is summarized in a letter which Bp. O'Connor wrote on March 4, 1852 and sent to the Society for the Propagation of the Faith in Paris, France:

> For the past two or three years we have suffered a persecution here in this city which is without comparison in our day in civilized nations. I do not know to what to attribute it, except that the progress of our holy religion seems to excite hate in impious men. The sects pursue us with a bitter hate, but that one can understand. Besides the sects properly so called, there is a class of men risen up here who call themselves "preachers on the streets." They do not care to claim any particular belief and they do not belong to any sect. They are for the most part men without character for whom no one has any respect and to whom no one would trust anything that he expected to be returned. Night and day they preach in the market places and on street corners where the public assembles. When I say "preach" I am merely using their words. That which they call "preaching" consists entirely in a series of insults the most infamous that one could say against us, against the clergy, the religious, and catholics in general. They relate with most revolting obscenity the doctrines of Michelet and Courier about the confessional. They misuse that which catholic theologians have written on every kind of sin, they read for everyone these passages and make very crude and revolting remarks about them with gestures, as they say, to make comprehensible what catholic theology is and what goes on in the confessional. They accuse all catholic women of prostitution, particularly the religious. They invent the grossest lies and tell them in full daylight. They check themselves from saying things that could be punished in the courts, at least they stop from saying things which we could carry there.

Things have gone so far during the last year that the mayor of the city, a son of a minister, had them brought before his court because of the obscenity of their discourse. The judge, the jury, everyone seemed united in condemning them. Their leader was condemned to a year in jail and fined $500. But his friends nevertheless proposed him for Mayor of the town and at the election which followed brought about his election. He was elected and installed as Mayor while he was yet a prisoner in jail; the Governor of the state being unwilling to oppose the voice of the majority let him get out. And that man so infamous, condemned by a jury on which none was Catholic, is the chief magistrate since last January.

That which gives power to these men is that in this city more than any other in the United States, we have a great number of Orange Irishmen. They persecute Catholics with bitterness and without shame. The more respectable Protestants condemn these men, but the Orangemen often manage matters so well they impose on some and seduce others and succeed in encouraging these apostles of impiety and obtaining for them a freedom from punishment.

What I fear is that these things will end in a riot. I am sure that that is what they desire and what they try to bring about. Up to the present time with the help of God we have succeeded in maintaining tranquility. For some weeks they have come every Sunday afternoon to give their discourses near the windows of the Seminary. They are accompanied by a crowd of desperate men who have no religion or morals and who wish nothing more than an excuse to attack us. They have the hope that Catholics will attack them.

It is the mayor himself who preaches on these occasions. Since he is the one who names the members of the police you can understand what our security is. Last Sunday a group of German women attacked them by throwing stones. It will be necessary for me to strive to prevent a repetition of this scene, otherwise we will have a repetition of the bloody riots of Philadelphia of 1844.

Our situation in these matters is truly frightful. Under the appearance of Liberty they labor to produce a state of things in which I am sure they would produce nothing less than to throw us out of the city as soon as they could obtain a pretext.

Michael O'Connor[28]

In October of 1854, Pius IX summoned Bp. O'Connor and Abp. Kenrick to Rome so that they could assist in the final examination and revision of the definition of the dogma of the Immaculate Conception of the Blessed Virgin Mary. Bp. O'Connor is credited with the formulation of a great part of the definition of the dogma. For this service he was honored by the Holy Father in being named an Assistant to the Pontifical Throne.[29]

The dedication of the second St. Paul Cathedral on June 24, 1855, was characterized by a solemn liturgy and celebration. Many members of the American hierarchy participated in the consecration of this magnificent structure at Fifth Avenue and Grant Street.

Bp. O'Connor was determined that the Cathedral would be dedicated in 1855, but he had to overcome a dilemma. Canon law prohibited the consecration of a structure until it was debt free. There was a $40,000 debt remaining on the cathedral. To circumvent the law, O'Connor temporarily transferred the debt to the property in Birmingham. This made it *appear* that the Cathedral was free of debt and eligible for consecration.

The demands upon a missionary bishop were numerous. They increased with time and the expansion of the diocese. Overseeing the construction of the Cathedral and managing the diocese taxed the mental and physical abilities of Bp. O'Connor. The bishop's health started to decline in 1853. He began to complain of severe headaches. Preaching became a struggle. His general health declined rapidly in 1855 and 1856. Since his physical appearance was not altered, physicians and priests were somewhat suspicious of O'Connor's constant headaches. The effects of stress on a person's physical condition was not then appreciated so they concluded that the ailments were imaginary.

Stress was a constant companion for Bp. O'Connor. In addition to the increase in population and the expansion of the Diocese, he had to contend with the goals and ambitions of Fr. Boniface Wimmer, O.S.B., as well as the complaints of some German priests and nuns. Tensions with persons and finances seemed to be perpetual.

O'Connor's physicians were unable to prescribe a cure for the bishop's illness and so they advised travel for the benefit of his health.

The new St. Paul Cathedral on Grant Street in downtown Pittsburgh was dedicated in 1855.

Accompanied by Fr. T.S. Reynolds, Bp. O'Connor sailed for Europe on December 10, 1856. Fr. Edward McMahon, the pastor of St. Paul Cathedral, was appointed administrator of the Diocese during O'Connor's absence.

O'Connor toured Europe, Egypt, and the Holy Land. He did not ignore his obligations. He lectured regularly and collected funds for the cathedral. The building debt was always on his mind. At the end of the tour, however, there was no apparent improvement in his health.

Realizing that because of his physical ailments the proper management of the Diocese was beyond his personal capabilities, Bp. O'Connor petitioned the Vatican for the appointment of a coadjutor. In response to his petition, two appointments were made, but both appointees rejected their selection.

Fr. John B. Byrne, pastor of St. Matthew Church, Washington, D.C., was appointed on May 9, 1857 to be coadjutor bishop of Pittsburgh. Even though the date for his ordination was set, Fr. Byrne withdrew unexpectedly from the appointment and then retired to Mount St. Mary's in Emmitsburg, Maryland. A second candidate, Fr. Edward Purcell, vicar-general, and brother of the archbishop of Cincinnati, also declined the same appointment.[30]

THE DIOCESE OF ERIE

In 1853 the Diocese of Erie was formed out of the Diocese of Pittsburgh. In the same year controversy continued over the establishment of St. Vincent's as an abbey.

Bp. O'Connor had recommended the division of the Diocese of Pittsburgh because he found that the northern area of the diocese was difficult to cover by parochial visitations. Although O'Connor offered to move to the new diocese, there was a strong suspicion that the division and the bishop's offer to transfer were the result of Benedictine pressure.

Abp. Kenrick wrote to his brother Peter, bishop of St. Louis: "I think it opportune for you to write to the sacred congregation about the transfer of our friend. This was done without any advice of the

Bishops of our country and as I suspect, to please the King of Bavaria, who asked the favor of the Holy Father in order to secure the Benedictines against the Bishop who opposed their making liquor out of grain and running a public tavern."[31]

Fr. James Bradley wrote to Fr. Thomas Heyden: "Our bishop has gone to Erie and report says he will soon be transferred to New York to be coadjutor to Archbishop Hughes whose health is declining. Dr. Young has declined Pittsburgh, and the Germans tried to get a German bishop."[32]

Bp. O'Connor transferred to Erie on October 14, 1853. Appointed to be Bp. O'Connor's successor, Fr. Josue Young, a convert to Catholicism, was reluctant to come to Pittsburgh. He felt inexperienced, and he knew that he would not be welcome because of disappointment at Bp. O'Connor's transfer.

The clergy and laity of the Diocese of Pittsburgh initiated a two-pronged attack on the transfer of Bp. O'Connor. They formed an organized effort to prevent O'Connor's departure, and they tried to induce Fr. Young to refuse the nomination.

Fr. Young complied with their desires and refused his appointment.

A solution to the dilemma was effected when on February 18, 1854, on the recommendation of Abp. Bedini, O'Connor was reappointed to the Diocese of Pittsburgh. Only then did Fr. Josue Young agree to accept appointment to the Diocese of Erie. He was ordained as the Bishop of Erie on April 23, 1854.[33]

Bp. O'Connor's health did not improve, and his doctors ordered him to spend the winter in a warmer climate. In October of 1857, he set out for the West Indies and Mexico. Again he devoted time and effort to collecting for St. Paul Cathedral. He returned to Pittsburgh on April 22, 1858.

The conviction that he was incapable of fulfilling his duties severely troubled Bp. O'Connor. Bp. Young of Erie was a willing assistant in visiting parishes and in administering the Sacrament of Confirmation. Still, O'Connor felt that he was neglecting his responsibilities. On July 16, 1859 he sailed for Rome with the intention of submitting his resignation. At the recommendation of Abp. Kenrick, he appointed his brother, Fr. James O'Connor, to serve as administrator of the Diocese.

While O'Connor was abroad, the cathedral residence was damaged by fire on November 3, 1859. Plans for a new residence, at the cost of $16,000, were quickly formulated. At his return the bishop rejected the plans. However, he did allow the construction of a brick front to camouflage the damaged building. He continued to live in the battered edifice.

In the spring of 1860, in an effort to keep his request to resign as secret as possible, Bp. O'Connor traveled to New York to send his message to Rome. This time his petition was granted on May 25, and the official document was received in New York on June 15. In the *Pittsburgh Catholic* of June 18, 1860, Bp. O'Connor published a short farewell message in which he explained that his continued illness forced this "painful measure" on him.[34] Again, Fr. James O'Connor was assigned to be the administrator of the Diocese until a new bishop could be appointed.

The 17-year tenure of Michael O'Connor has been favorably viewed by historians. In his *History of the Catholic Church In The United States*, John Gilmary Shea classifies Michael O'Connor as "one of the glories of the American Church."[35] This description was richly deserved. While still a young man of 31, he undertook the tremendous task of forming a vast diocese with a minimum of clergy. The speed with which he organized the Diocese of Pittsburgh is indicative of O'Connor's abilities and talents.

In 1843, when O'Connor arrived in Pittsburgh, the Catholics of western Pennsylvania were few in number, poor, a political and social minority. The enormity of the mission might have taxed a man of lesser ability and dedication. The glory of God and the welfare of his flock were always first in O'Connor's thoughts. His great success was due primarily to the selflessness which motivated all his actions up to and including his illness.

Bp. Michael O'Connor was an extraordinary man. He was truly a scholar. As a linguist, he could speak and understand Latin, Greek, Hebrew, Irish, French, German, Italian and English. He had a keen mind and excellent knowledge of religious doctrine and the strength of logic.

When Abp. Bedini filed the report of his visit to the United States, he rated Bp. O'Connor: "second only to Archbishop Hughes as a leader of his flock and as an orator."[36]

O'Connor had great success in gaining clergy and religious to labor in the Diocese. He had strong motivations to increase the numbers of priests and sisters. He was impelled constantly to meet the ordinary religious needs of Catholics. The predominance of Protestants and Protestant thought made him especially sensitive to the possibility of unattended Catholics losing their faith.

As a writer, Bp. O'Connor was a frequent contributor to the *Pittsburgh Catholic* and that remains the chief source of his writings.

Bp. O'Connor was a strong advocate for religious education for everyone. He made appeals before the Pennsylvania Legislature on behalf of Catholic education. In 1853, he appealed unsuccessfully for a share of public funds for Catholic Schools because the School Laws of 1834 empowered district school directors to distribute tax funds to religious schools.

The genius of Bp. O'Connor was that he had a zeal for the active ministry. He was constant in visiting and caring for the people of the Diocese.

Serious obligations in diocesan management and pressures from government officials were fertile ground for a person to make some mistakes. For all his abilities and patience, there were occasions when O'Connor was too hasty in his reactions, and obstinate in his decisions.

His enthusiasm to establish and maintain a seminary required that the students move from one location to another, which created an instability in their formation. Also, the withdrawal of the Sisters of Charity from their work in the Diocese appears to have resulted from O'Connor's insistence that he was in charge of all organizations within the diocese.

His battles with Boniface Wimmer, O.S.B., were due to the clash of two dominant personalities, each insisting on personal rights and privileges. O'Connor's disagreements with Fr. Wimmer and other German priests over the use of funds received from Germany deprived the Diocese of the financial support of the Ludwig-Missionverein of Bavaria.

Personality conflicts also fueled the political disaster that arose when

O'Connor tried to obtain a coadjutor. His precipitous decision to form the Diocese of Erie was an indication of his excessive haste.

O'Connor showed favoritism to his younger brother, Fr. James O'Connor. The appointment of his brother as administrator of the Diocese in his absence damaged his esteem among diocesan priests and produced opposition from the clergy during his final years in office.

Bp. O'Connor had a real love for oratory. When the Know-Nothing party and Mayor Joe Barker were making life miserable for Catholics in Pittsburgh, O'Connor, on March 17, 1852 delivered a two-hour lecture in the Masonic Hall in Pittsburgh. The topic of his discourse was: "The influence of Catholicity on the civil institutions of the United States — The motives and necessity of this influence." Reaction to this lecture required a further response to O'Connor's critics. On April 21, he proved the depth of his knowledge of theology, philosophy, and the history of English political institutions. O'Connor concluded his lecture with a prediction: "Yet the day may come, when it will be found that this despised Catholicity will be the safeguard of the Republic."[37]

After his resignation and before he joined the Jesuits, O'Connor lectured in New York City for the benefit of Pittsburgh's diocesan seminary. These talks were a financial boost toward the elimination of the seminary debt.

O'Connor's 17-year tenure was most productive. He organized a vast territory into a very practical diocese. A singular achievement was his founding of the *Pittsburgh Catholic*. Since its first issue on March 16, 1844, it is the oldest continuously published Catholic newspaper in the United States.

The effectiveness of Bishop O'Connor's term can also be measured in sheer numbers. When he assumed the leadership of the Diocese of Pittsburgh in 1843, there were 33 churches. When he left, there were 77. Under his leadership, the number of priests rose from 21 to 86, and the number of seminarians increased from 8 to 30. O'Connor worked to maintain four orphanages for boys and two for girls. In 1860, five male and three female religious orders were established and active in the Diocese.

O'CONNOR AND THE JESUITS

Resignation from the office of bishop induced some improvement in O'Connor's health, but it did not end the discipleship of the dedicated cleric.

When O'Connor asked to be relieved of his duties as bishop, he begged the pope to retract his ability to administer the Sacrament of Confirmation. Pius IX agreed. This unusual petition resulted from O'Connor's desire to retain a degree of anonymity as he pursued his longtime desire to join the Society of Jesus.

He sought seclusion, leaving the United States and entering the Jesuit Novitiate at Gorheim, Sigmaringen, Germany on December 22, 1860. One day, while offering Mass, he inadvertently betrayed his former position by greeting fellow novices with the bishop's salutation: "Pax Vobis" (Peace be with you), instead of the priest's: "Dominus Vobiscum" (The Lord be with you).

The Jesuit vows of poverty, chastity, obedience, and special obedience to the pope are ordinarily pronounced at separate ceremonies with a time lapse between the first three and the fourth. After a two-year novitiate, O'Connor received special dispensation to make the four vows in a single ceremony on December 23, 1862, at Boston, Massachusetts.

During his first year as a Jesuit, O'Connor taught theology at Boston College. In the following year, he was selected to be the *Socius* (Companion) to the Jesuit Provincial, who profited from O'Connor's knowledge and experience. O'Connor's skills were of great assistance to the Provincial. While fulfilling these duties O'Connor lived at Loyola College in Baltimore, Maryland. He was extremely busy as a preacher, lecturer and retreat master.

ADVOCATE FOR AFRICAN-AMERICANS

From the earliest days of his priesthood, one goal had eluded Fr. O'Connor. He always manifested a great zeal for the welfare and religious training of African-American Catholics. He was bishop of Pittsburgh only a few months when he started a Chapel of the Nativity for African-American Catholics. This venture, unfortunately, was short-lived, but it evidenced an interest that remained to the end of his life.

While living in Baltimore and holding an influential position in the Society of Jesus, he brought his goal to fruition. In 1863, he spent time securing funds and a church to establish the first African-American parish in the United States, St. Francis Xavier Church, Baltimore, Maryland.

O'Connor became the liaison who united the efforts of two very dedicated priests — Abp. Martin Spalding of Baltimore and Fr. Herbert Vaughan of London, England. Spalding was committed to encouraging Catholic evangelization among African-Americans. Vaughan had established St. Joseph's Society of the Sacred Heart for foreign missions.

O'Connor convinced the two priests that Vaughan's missionaries should come to Baltimore to work among African-Americans. In 1871, he also persuaded his Jesuit superiors to transfer St. Francis Xavier Church to the Mill Hill Fathers, Fr. Vaughan's missionaries from St. Joseph Seminary in the Mill Hill section of London. Since 1893 these missionaries are known in the United States by their proper name: *The Society of St. Joseph of the Sacred Heart*, and are popularly called the Josephites.

St. Francis Xavier parish in Baltimore and the community it served remained in Fr. O'Connor's interest until his death at Woodstock College in Maryland, in 1872. The Josephites, whose chief mission is to serve African-Americans, consider Michael O'Connor to be their American sponsor.[38]

EXEMPLARY PIONEER PRIESTS

Before and after the founding of the Diocese of Pittsburgh, two priests served as exemplary representatives of the clergy and the church during a period of transition.

From the First Synod of the Diocese of Pittsburgh in 1844, in which they both held important posts, until their deaths in the latter half of the nineteenth century, Frs. Thomas Heyden and James Stillinger were admired and consulted by clerics, religious and laity.

THOMAS HEYDEN

Thomas Heyden was born in 1798 in County Carlow, Ireland. As an infant he was brought to America by his parents, who operated a small store in Bedford, Bedford County, Pennsylvania.

After being educated in Bedford schools, he enrolled at Mt. St. Mary College in Emmitsburg, Maryland. He was, and continued to be throughout his life, a diligent student. He progressed so rapidly that a dispensation from the canonical age of 24 had to be obtained for his ordination on May 21, 1821.

Except for brief stints at St. Joseph and St. Mary churches in Philadelphia, and at St. Paul Church in Pittsburgh, Heyden spent his entire life as a priest at St. Thomas Church in Bedford.

Although he was extremely popular with parishioners, Heyden was a retiring man who loved to study. He became, with some reticence, a leader among the clergy of the Diocese. He rejected an appointment as bishop of Natchez, Mississippi but was often proposed as a qualified episcopal candidate for Pittsburgh and other dioceses.

Fr. Heyden was a friend and confidant of Bp. O'Connor, but he also was a leading advocate for the clergy when he thought any mistreatment or inconsiderate practices had occurred. He was deeply concerned about the welfare of the Diocese and the Church. He did not hesitate to express his concerns in writing, and this correspondence (now in the Pittsburgh diocesan archives) reveals much about the early days of the Diocese of Pittsburgh.

Fr. Heyden was in the fiftieth year of his priesthood when he died, August 25, 1870.

JAMES STILLINGER

James Stillinger was born in Baltimore, Maryland on April 19, 1801. There are no records of his immediate family. He was reared by a grandfather who died when James was 11 years old.

At that young age, Stillinger was on his own, doing odd jobs and attending school whenever possible. At 16, he was employed by a German printer. While learning to set type, Stillinger also acquired a fluency in German. Afterwards, he was employed as an apprentice at a printing shop in Gettysburg, Adams County, Pennsylvania.

On Sunday mornings, he would travel many miles to attend Mass at various churches. On one of these excursions he met Fr. John Dubois of Mount Saint Mary College. Dubois, who later became bishop of New York, encouraged Stillinger to pursue a vocation to the priesthood. He continued to counsel and assist him in achieving that goal.

In November 1820, Stillinger entered Mount St. Mary College. He was ordained a priest there on February 28, 1830. For the next few months he lived at the College, serving the college church and the church at Liberty, Frederick County, Maryland.

In November 1830, he was assigned to Sportsman's Hall and to Blairsville, both in Westmoreland County. He rescued the Sportsman's Hall parish from the lingering effects of Frs. Cause and Fromm, and developed it into an active community. He even planned the founding of a Catholic school at the site of the present St. Vincent College.

Fr. Stillinger became a confidant and advisor to bishops, priests and laity. Bp. O'Connor appointed him as his first vicar-general in the Diocese of Pittsburgh. His solid priestly virtues of piety, prudence and zeal appealed to all the clergy and laity of the Diocese.

Fr. Stillinger died in Blairsville on September 19, 1873.

Bishop Michael Domenec

Five

Michael Domenec, C.M.
1860–1876
Second Bishop of Pittsburgh

Michael Domenec was born at Reus, near Tarragona, Spain on December 27, 1816. He studied in public, private and religious institutions in Reus until the age of 16, when his family, for political reasons, was forced to flee to France.

Domenec attended the College of Montolieu in Adus, France. He joined the Congregation of the Missions, popularly known as the Vincentians, and lived at the motherhouse in Paris, France.

The novitiate training for the Vincentians was rigorous. During this time of preparation, Domenec formed attitudes that became the foundation of his priesthood. His primary spiritual motivation was absolute devotion to the will of God. He maintained a firm belief in the presence of God being with him always, and he submitted all activities to the judgment of God. His goal was to live in God's presence and to do God's will so that he might satisfy God's judgment.

These attitudes gave rise to Domenec's calm, prayerful character, which, combined with his native Spanish charm, produced a polished gentleman.

In 1837, while Michael Domenec was still a seminarian and theology student, Father John Timon, C.M., came from the Vincentian Seminary at Barrens, Missouri to the motherhouse in Paris. His purpose was to solicit funds for the seminary in the United States. He also appealed for missionaries to the United States. When Timon returned to America, he was accompanied by Domenec.

After he enrolled in the seminary at Barrens on February 10, 1838, Domenec was ordained a subdeacon by Bishop Joseph Rosati, C.M., in 1838. When he was ordained on June 30, 1839, Domenec was the youngest priest in the United States.[1]

For six years, Fr. Michael Domenec worked as a missionary and served as seminary director in southeastern Missouri. When the Vincentians were asked to take charge of St. Charles Borromeo Seminary in Philadelphia, in 1845, Domenec went there and joined the faculty. In addition to his teaching, he continued to work as a missionary at St. James Parish in Nicetown. In 1847, he was assigned to begin St. Vincent DePaul Church in Germantown.

After acquiring a reputation as a zealous, hard-working and successful pastor, Fr. Domenec was chosen to be the second bishop of Pittsburgh in 1860. Initially, he objected to this appointment, but later he reluctantly accepted the office.[2]

The atmosphere in the Diocese of Pittsburgh was hardly ideal. Clerics were antagonized by the decisions of Fr. James O'Connor, the younger brother of Bp. O'Connor, who had served as the administrator of the Diocese until Bp. Domenec was ordained.

Fr. O'Connor's youth and inexperience made him unpopular with the clergy, who feared he would become their bishop. During the time that Fr. O'Connor was in charge of the Diocese, a fire damaged a large part of the cathedral residence. Asserting his authority, he promoted the immediate construction of a new residence (at the cost of $16,000) and the remodeling of the parish school.

Many of the clergy opposed Fr. O'Connor's plans. O'Connor responded by suspending Fr. John Tuigg, whom he suspected to be a leader of the diocesan priests. Fr. Tuigg was exonerated, and the incident did not prevent him from later becoming the third bishop of Pittsburgh.

The opposition to the administration of Fr. James O'Connor caused a breach of clerical etiquette when Domenec arrived in Pittsburgh. No one was at the train station to welcome him to the cathedral. A flood of apologies followed. Domenec, who had a genial disposition, did not dwell on the discourtesy.

Domenec had been appointed bishop of Pittsburgh on September 23, 1860. He was ordained by Archbishop Francis Kenrick in St. Paul Cathedral on December 9, 1860.[3]

That year was a watershed for the nation. Abraham Lincoln had been elected president, and the Civil War was imminent. Pittsburgh was not exempt from those tensions and was soon involved in an armed scrimmage.

On Christmas Day 1860, two weeks after Domenec's ordination, Pittsburgh newspapers reported that the United States Secretary of War, John B. Floyd of Virginia, had ordered more than 100 cannons shipped from the Allegheny Arsenal in Lawrenceville to locations in southern states.

War had not been declared but it was obvious that these cannons might soon be used against Union forces. For more than a week, the local citizenry armed themselves and resisted the transport of these guns by the militia. Residents of Pittsburgh threatened to sink the steamboat "Silver Wave" if it left its Monongahela River port. This citizen's response constituted armed resistance to an order by the federal government. Early in January of 1861, Attorney General Edwin M. Stanton rescinded Secretary Floyd's order and the cannons were not shipped to the Confederacy.

Traditionally, the attack on Fort Sumter on April 11, 1861 is considered the first battle of the Civil War. But three months before the combat, Pittsburghers won what was really the first skirmish in the battle to preserve the Union.[4]

Domenec was a strong supporter of the Union. At the outbreak of the war, he asked for a triduum of prayer and a special Mass for the preservation of the Union. He ordered that the nation's flag be flown at the cathedral and he preached frequently about the civic obligations of Catholics.

In spite of these frequent professions of fealty to the Union, the local press never missed an opportunity to print rumors regarding disloyal Catholics and their divided allegiance. On occasion, expressions of loyalty to the South by Southern clergy were distorted and applied to all Catholic priests. Such appeals to bigotry always aroused enmity toward the Catholic Church.

Bp. Domenec remained loyal to the Union cause, and he performed a successful diplomatic mission on behalf of its forces.

By the Treaty of London of October 21, 1861, the nations of Great Britain, France and Spain indicated their sympathy with the cause of the Confederacy because they were concerned about their shipping interest with Mexico. To counteract this attitude, United States Secretary of State William H. Seward appealed to Abp. John Hughes of New York to visit these countries on behalf of the Union.

An opportunity to fulfill this request was found when Hughes was in Europe to attend the canonization of the martyrs of Japan in April 1862. Bp. Domenec also went to Rome for this solemn occasion. Abp. Hughes called upon officials in England and France. When Hughes became ill, he asked Domenec, who planned to go to Spain, to intercede with Spanish officials on behalf of the North.

After Domenec visited his mother, he went to Lisbon and was received by Calderone de Collantes, the foreign minister of Spain, and Leopold O'Donnell, a Spanish military leader. Hughes later remarked that Bishop Domenec "really succeeded" in his mission. Spain remained neutral throughout the war.[5]

Although the actual fighting was still at a distance, in June 1863 the city of Pittsburgh was fortified because many believed the rebels contemplated capturing it. The Allegheny Arsenal in Lawrenceville was a principal manufactory of munitions for the Union Army and would be a potential target. Whatever its cause, a violent explosion had occurred at the Allegheny Arsenal on September 17, 1862. Seventy-eight people were killed, and hundreds of workers were injured.

ADMINISTRATIVE CHANGES

When he began work, Bp. Domenec retained all of the diocesan officials. Fr. Edward McMahon, chancellor, and Fr. James O'Connor, rector of the seminary, were his vicars-general. This convenient practice relieved him of administrative details and permitted him to concentrate on pastoral ministry. As Domenec traveled from parish to parish to administer the Sacrament of Confirmation, he ingratiated himself with members of the Diocese.

Although he had been reluctant to assume the office of bishop, Domenec was so determined to perform God's will that he became an exemplary bishop. He won the affection of clergy and laity by the way he entered into all the duties and functions of the church in the Diocese of Pittsburgh.

When Domenec placed complete confidence in his predecessor's staff without learning the details of diocesan finances, however, he made a serious error in judgment. These officials decided the new bishop was a poor administrator and "unfit for the episcopacy." The bishop's secretary, Fr. James Keogh, sent critical reports on Bp. Domenec's executive ability to the Vatican.[6] Frs. Edward McMahon and James O'Connor shared Keogh's opinion. These priests had been leaders of the clerical faction that supported Bp. O'Connor.

Fr. Keogh, a protege of Bp. O'Connor, was a brilliant priest. He was a capable secretary and served as editor of the *Pittsburgh Catholic*. As editor, Keogh sometimes was a source of embarrassment to Bp. Domenec. Priests complained that his editorials were too political for a diocesan newspaper, but Domenec was loath to dismiss him. It was the bishop's inclination always to be gentle, but this lack of forcefulness in dealing with problems was one of his major weaknesses.

After his first year as bishop, Domenec became alarmed by the finances of the cathedral and the seminary. An inability to support clergy of the Diocese (who needed financial help) caused disagreements between the bishop and his officials. Domenec's first reaction to this discord was to resign, but Abp. Kenrick persuaded him to change his mind.[7]

To gain control over the administration, Domenec made additional appointments to his diocesan council in 1862. This move caused Fr. McMahon to resign as chancellor while retaining the rectorship of the cathedral. In his resignation, he stated that he felt he was now "unnecessary" to the Diocese.[8]

A year later, in December of 1863, without prior notice, Domenec revoked all ecclesiastical offices and positions that required his appointment and sanction. These vacancies were filled by new appointees on January 2, 1864.

With these changes, Bp. Domenec obtained knowledge and control of diocesan finances. At the same time, he doubled the number of diocesan deaneries from two to four and appointed a vicar-general for German parishes.

The pro-O'Connor faction of the Pittsburgh clergy objected to the abrupt changes in the administration, but an appeal to Vatican officials was fruitless. Rome's response was that this method was not unprecedented because diocesan officials do not have lifetime appointments.

Moreover, a survey of the diocesan clergy indicated that 79 of the 94 priests approved of the changes in diocesan administration. They agreed that the changes were made to meet diocesan needs and were not the result of Domenec's personal prejudice. Bp. O'Connor, in a letter to his brother James on January 20, 1864, supported the changes and stated that his successor had "acted justly."[9]

Soon afterward, Frs. James O'Connor and James Keogh resigned, and together with Fr. McMahon, they transferred to the Diocese of Philadelphia.

In Domenec's new administration, Frs. Tobias Mullen, who later became bishop of Erie, and John Steibel were appointed vicars-general.

Fr. John Hickey was appointed chancellor and secretary to Domenec. Domenec was especially pleased with this last appointment. He wrote to Fr. Heyden on January 9, 1864 that there was "No one better fit for my secretary and chancellor under my present circumstances than Fr. Hickey."[10]

PASTORAL MINISTRY

During the Civil War, Bp. Domenec derived great consolation from pastoral ministry. He frequently traveled throughout the Diocese to preach, administer the sacraments, lecture and attend ceremonies. His spirit of service and self-sacrifice was admired by all and his reputation grew in esteem and popularity.

Each year, Domenec administered the Sacrament of Confirmation in every parish. He also directed retreats and missions. Sometimes he would remain as long as eight days in a small town and meet each member of the parish.

On September 11, 1862, after Domenec had made a pastoral visit to St. John Parish in Altoona, Fr. John Tuigg wrote to Fr. Thomas Heyden: "With his usual kindness he consented to preach at the dedication."[11]

The Pittsburgh area was a lively center for Civil War activity. The city was strategically located. The Allegheny arsenal was essential for the production of material for warfare. The railroads and rivers that ran through Pittsburgh helped the city develop into a manufacturing center.

The draft law of the federal government did not exempt priests from military service. Clergy who were drafted could serve in a hospital or in an institution to take care of freed men. A third option, available to anyone who could afford it, was to pay $300 to the government. The $300 was the stipulated sum for the support of a substitute in military service. Nine priests of the Diocese of Pittsburgh were drafted, but they were excused from service because their parishes contributed the fee for a substitute.

Families of soldiers were often in dire need, and Bp. Domenec was anxious to assist them. The Societies of St. Vincent DePaul, introduced into the Diocese by Bp. O'Connor in 1852, were now established in every parish.

On October 27, 1861, Domenec instituted an official Particular Council of the St. Vincent DePaul Society to oversee and coordinate assistance wherever it was needed. He also encouraged and cooperated with the municipal Committee of Public Safety for the alleviation of the needs of all people.

MICHAEL J. O'CONNOR'S PENSION

In addition to administrative housecleaning and wartime efforts, Domenec engaged in an aggravating duel with his predecessor, Bp. Michael O'Connor, over the matter of O'Connor's pension.

After his resignation, Bp. O'Connor became obsessed with fears of illness. It was this nagging illness that had prompted him to relinquish his post as bishop.

The first referee of O'Connor's pension was Abp. Francis Kenrick.

He offered O'Connor $500 annually, and also proposed that whatever estate the retired bishop might leave be managed by his successor. O'Connor was not satisfied and wrote to Kenrick on July 10, 1860 that he disliked "being at the mercy and whim of a future bishop."[12]

When Domenec was in Europe in 1862, he met with O'Connor in Marseilles, France, and they agreed to alter Kenrick's plan. Their agreement, however, did not solve the problem. Bp. O'Connor continued to vacillate on the management of his estate. He complicated matters by stipulating a donation to the Sisters of Mercy and then prescribing complicated methods in the distribution of this donation.

Bp. Domenec made his mistake by failing to insist that the arrangements be made in writing. These misunderstandings over O'Connor's wishes regarding the distribution of his estate caused strained relationships between the two men as well as with Fr. James O'Connor, who often represented his brother in the negotiations. Finally, Abp. James F. Wood of Philadelphia replaced James O'Connor in the transactions and devised a solution that included gifts to the Diocese of Pittsburgh from Bp. O'Connor's estate.

NUNS OF THE BATTLEFIELD

The *Congressional Record* of March 18, 1918 comments: "The early histories of the Civil War are full of praises for the noble women, many of whom lost their health and lives tending the sick and the wounded." This item is contained in a detailed account of the Catholic nuns who served as nurses during the Civil War.[13]

In our nation's capital there is a monument called *Nuns of the Battlefield*. The statue was erected across the street from St. Matthew Church as public tribute to the more than 800 Catholic sisters who volunteered to care for the sick and wounded immediately behind the lines. The sisters opened their hearts and homes to the sick, wounded and dying of both Union and Confederate forces.

These sisters gave devoted service under the most difficult conditions. Their hospitals were warehouses or barns and sanitation was almost impossible. The work of the sisters was the only organized nursing during the Civil War. The Nurses Corps and the Red Cross were not established until after the war.

The sisters were called upon to do more than nurse the wounded. Catholic chaplains were very scarce. As a result, the sisters often had to fulfill their role as well. Theodore Maynard observed: "Often, after having made all efforts to save life, they had to show men how to die."[14]

The dedication demonstrated by these sisters did much to break down bigotry and antagonism towards the Catholic Church.

Twenty-nine officers of high rank in the Union Army, and fourteen in the Confederate Army, entered the Church during and after the Civil War.[15] "All these sisters must be remembered for their heroic service in the cause of charity. And they must still be more remembered on account of their service to a better understanding of the Church and all it stands for; no one who experienced their unselfish charity could long remain a bigot."[16]

Some of these sisters were from the Diocese of Pittsburgh. In November 1862, Bp. Domenec notified the superior of the Sisters of Mercy, Sr. Rose Hostetter, that he had offered the services of her order to the Secretary of War, Edwin A. Stanton. The war secretary acted quickly; four sisters from Mercy Hospital were summoned to action on November 25, 1862. Soon afterwards, four more sisters followed.

At least eight sisters from Pittsburgh served throughout the war at Stanton Hospital in Washington, D.C., and others provided nursing care at the Western Pennsylvania Military Hospital, the military designation for Mercy Hospital.

In her book, *Nuns of the Battlefield*, Ellen Ryan Jolly quotes a beautiful tribute to these sisters by President Abraham Lincoln:

> Of all the forms of charity and benevolence seen in the crowded wards of the hospitals, those of some Catholic sisters were among the most efficient. I never knew whence they came or what was the name of their Order. More lovely than anything I had ever seen in art, so long devoted to illustrations of love, mercy and charity, are the pictures that remain of these modest sisters going on their errands of mercy among the suffering and dying. Gentle and womanly, yet with the courage of soldiers leading a forlorn hope, to sustain them in contact with such horrors. As they went from cot to cot, distributing the medicines prescribed, administering the cooling, refreshing draughts as directed, they were veritable Angels of Mercy.[17]

THE SISTERS OF MERCY

The Sisters of Mercy came to the Diocese of Pittsburgh with Bp. O'Connor in 1843. During his tenure they were favored by the bishop and by his brother, Fr. James O'Connor, who had been their superior for several years. When Bp. Domenec clashed with the O'Connors, the Sisters of Mercy sided with and supported them.

As a Vincentian, Domenec regarded his duty as supervisor of female religious communities within his diocese as a serious obligation. Bishop O'Connor's supervision was one of friendly cooperation, but Domenec maintained a more direct and arbitrary method of domination over the nuns.

The Sisters of Mercy was the largest community of nuns in the Diocese. They had nine institutions, located in four of the counties of the Diocese.

Bp. Domenec became displeased with the superior of the Sisters of Mercy, Sr. Mechtildes O'Connell, R.S.M., because she did not consult with him on assignment of individual sisters. He was disturbed also by the practice of sisters teaching boys over twelve years of age, and that the Mercy Rule regarding visitors to the convent was not observed at St. Xavier's. He also maintained that the governmental structure of a single motherhouse supervising nine institutions did not conform with the practice of the Sisters of Mercy in Ireland, where each foundation was autonomous.

On July 14, 1874, Bp. Domenec called a meeting of the Sisters of Mercy at their motherhouse at St. Xavier Academy. He announced to the assembled sisters that he was going to separate each residence of the sisters. This meant that those residing at St. Mary's in Pittsburgh; St. Xavier's in Latrobe; St. Aloysius Academy in Cresson; at Mercy Hospital in Pittsburgh; and at the House of Industry in Allegheny would become separate communities. The bishop also claimed the right to assign individual sisters to whichever house he chose. He then appointed the superiors for each house.

At this meeting the bishop deprived the sisters of control over their internal affairs. He had suspended the election of superiors and confused the disposition of community properties.

The sisters were not accustomed to such discourteous treatment. Even though the bishop had concluded his decision with a demand for obedience, the sisters decided to fight back. They immediately contacted their friend, Fr. James O'Connor, then a parish priest in Philadelphia. He came to Pittsburgh and advised the sisters to write a complaint to Cardinal Alessandro Franchi, the Prefect of the Congregation of the Propagation of the Faith, which had charge of the Church in the United States. Mother Mechtildes O'Connell sent three letters composed by Fr. O'Connor to Cardinal Franchi. Unfortunately, parts of these letters went beyond the complaints and made some rash accusations against the character of Bp. Domenec.

In becoming an advocate for the Sisters of Mercy, Fr. O'Connor ignored and usurped the duties of Fr. William Pollard, who was in charge of religious communities. The accusation that Domenec had exceeded his jurisdiction by his action against the sisters was contradicted by the Charter Book of the Sisters of Mercy, which in 1852 granted absolute powers in the government of the sisters to the bishop of the Diocese in which the sisters resided. Domenec possessed the authority to enact his propositions. However, rather than focusing on his authority over the religious of the Diocese, this quarrel with the sisters became a conflict of personalities.[18]

Cardinal Franchi commissioned Msgr. Cesare Roncetti (who was in the Unites States on other business) and Bp. Patrick Lynch of Charleston, South Carolina to investigate the charges of personal misconduct on the part of Bp. Domenec. Those charges could not be substantiated. Bp. Domenec's plan to disrupt the Mercy community was to be held in abeyance until the cardinal could deal with the appeal filed in Rome.

The impetus for dividing the convents of the Sisters of Mercy was a request, made in 1874, by the sisters at St. Aloysius Academy, asking that they be detached from the motherhouse so that they could become an autonomous community. Their goal was achieved when they became an independent community in 1879.

The Sisters of Mercy were not the only religious community to be subjected to the authoritarian methods of Bp. Domenec. The division of the Diocese, with the erection of the Diocese of Allegheny in 1875,

Bishop John F. Dearden prays at the tomb of Bishop Michael Domenec at Tarragona, Spain during a 1958 visit.

involved the Benedictine Sisters, the Sisters of Charity and Domenec's plan concerning the assignments of sisters. The basis for these conflicts was the location of motherhouses and convents in different dioceses.

PAPAL INFALLIBILITY

Pope Pius IX (1846–1878) had a long, turbulent papacy. In 1864, he began consultations regarding the propriety of invoking a General Council. In 1868, he notified the hierarchies throughout the world that there would be an Ecumenical Council at the Vatican in 1870.

The Council was to convene on December 8, 1869. A departure ceremony in Pittsburgh, conducted as Bp. Domenec was leaving for the Vatican Council, was one of the glorious events in his life. Clergy and laity expressed their love and appreciation as their spiritual leader departed for Rome to participate in discussions with prelates from every nation.

At the Council, Domenec did not have a prominent role. He received more notoriety after the Council than while he was a participant. He consistently supported minority opinions. In discussions on the feasibility of a declaration on infallibility, Domenec sided with the opposition. Domenec was not opposed to the doctrine of infallibility, but he agreed with Abp. Peter Kenrick of St. Louis in maintaining that it was the wrong time for such a definition. He argued that the topic of infallibility was a promotion by European media rather than from within the Council. Domenec feared that misconceptions of a definition of the infallibility of the pope would interfere with conversions to Catholicism in the United States.

At the final Council session on July 18, 1870, only two bishops voted against the definition of infallibility. Bp. Domenec was among a group of bishops who absented themselves from the last public session at which the vote was taken. As a result of this absence, Bishop Domenec's loyalty to the pope became suspect, and he was forced to submit a formal declaration of acceptance of all the decrees of the First Vatican Council.[19]

Pope Pius IX prepared commemorative medals to be presented to the bishops who participated in the Council. Abp. Martin Spalding of

Baltimore was to present these medals to the American bishops. Two of these medals were to be withheld, however, until specific conditions were met — Abp. Peter Kenrick and Bp. Michael Domenec were not to receive their medals until they formally assented to the decrees promulgated by the Council.[20]

When he returned to Pittsburgh at the conclusion of the Vatican Council, Bishop Domenec immediately preached and wrote about its decrees. He promulgated all of its declarations, but he also had to make a formal affirmation of his acceptance of all its decrees.

THE OBLATES OF SAINT CHARLES BORROMEO

In January 1870, two young priests and a brother came to Pittsburgh from England to establish a house of the Oblates of St. Charles Borromeo. They named their house, in the East Liberty district of the city, Our Lady of Victories. The limited sources of income by the small community were insufficient to meet the financial obligations of maintaining their foundation, and the project had to be abandoned before the end of the year.[21]

The failure of this venture is not as significant as the personalities of the two priests who were its founders. Both were from very prominent Pittsburgh families, and both were aspirants to the Protestant ministry. They had traveled to England to prepare themselves for service in the Presbyterian Church. Pursuing their studies, they eventually became converts to the Catholic Faith and continued their spiritual odyssey until they were ordained in the priesthood.

At a time when religious intolerance was prevalent in Pittsburgh and the Catholic Church was despised by many persons, their conversions to Catholicism and their ordination as priests was a shock to Pittsburgh society, primarily because their families were prominent in social and political circles.

Harmar Denny, born in Pittsburgh on June 15, 1833, was the grandson of the first mayor in Pittsburgh, Ebenezer Denny. His maternal grandfather was James O'Hara, the very successful entrepreneur in the development of Pittsburgh's industries. After completing his studies in Pittsburgh, Harmar Denny enrolled at Miami University in Oxford, Ohio. He then attended Princeton University. In 1855, he and his friend Pollard McCormick Morgan sailed for England to attend Oxford University to study for the ministry.

At Oxford, Harmar Denny decided to prepare for the Anglican ministry. Soon after this decision, he was introduced to Dr. Henry Edward Manning of the Oblates of Charles Borromeo. Catholic doctrines on infallibility, devotion to Mary, and priestly celibacy — which Harmar Denny considered to be insuperable difficulties — were soon answered satisfactorily by Dr. Manning. In 1857, he joined the Catholic Church and began studies for the priesthood.

In October of 1858, Harmar Denny transferred to the English College at Rome. On November 1, 1860, he was ordained a priest by Bishop Morris at St. Mary of the Angels at Bayswater, London, England.

In 1867 Harmar Denny conceived the idea of establishing a congregation of Oblates in America. At this time, he met Bp. Domenec in Rome and suggested his plan to the bishop. Domenec favored the idea, and Fr. Denny came to Pittsburgh. Until preparations could be made, Denny served as a chaplain at Mercy Hospital. In January 1870, he and his friend, Fr. Pollard Morgan, started Our Lady of Victories Oratory in East Liberty. Because of their meager sources of income, the priests assisted at St. James Church in Wilkinsburg, but they had to abandon their project within the year.

Fr. Denny consulted with Dr. Manning and Fr. Michael O'Connor, S.J., former bishop of Pittsburgh, about becoming a Paulist or a Jesuit. He then made his decision and on April 5, 1871, Fr. Denny began the process of becoming a Jesuit. Until his death at Woodstock, Maryland, on September 4, 1908, Fr. Denny was a very prominent preacher and retreat master.

Pollard McCormick Morgan was born in 1834. His father was an administrator at the Allegheny Arsenal in Lawrenceville. His paternal grandfather's property near Canonsburg was the area known as Morganza, for many years the site and title of a state school for delinquents.

Pollard Morgan attended city schools before enrolling at Western Theological Seminary, then located in Allegheny, where he studied to become a Presbyterian minister.

In 1855 he made a trip to Europe with his friend, Harmar Denny. His experiences in England and in Rome led him to join the Catholic Church. Upon his return to Pittsburgh, he became a seminarian at St. Michael Seminary, then located in Glenwood, near Hazelwood. He was ordained in Saint Paul Cathedral by Bp. Domenec on February 7, 1863. Fr. Morgan served at Brownsville, Loretto and at the seminary. He traveled to England to visit Fr. Harmar Denny in 1866. In a short time, after receiving permission from the Bp. Domenec, he joined the Oblates of Saint Charles Borromeo.

While awaiting the foundation of the Oratory in East Liberty, Fr. Morgan was assigned to St. Andrew Church in the Manchester district in Allegheny. When the Oratory failed, he returned to the diocesan clergy. Never very robust, his health failed and he died on April 14, 1872. At his funeral, in Saint Paul Cathedral, the homily was delivered by Fr. Harmar Denny, S.J.[22]

Six

John Tuigg
1876–1889
Third Bishop of Pittsburgh

The transition from Bishop Domenec to Bishop Tuigg was marred, for almost two years, by the ill-advised division of the Diocese and by financial problems. The establishment of the Allegheny Diocese and the monetary discord that ensued form a sad chapter in the history of the Diocese of Pittsburgh.

The Civil War, while destructive to the nation as a whole, was an industrial boon to the Pittsburgh area. The postwar years had been good financially, and Pittsburghers were not prepared for the deprivations brought on by the Panic of '73. The Diocese of Pittsburgh was especially hard hit by the depression. Many churches and institutions were being constructed or renovated and were burdened with serious debts.

The division of the Diocese, as recommended by Bp. Domenec, was especially problematic. The management of the Diocese was cumbersome, and it was evident that it should be reduced in size. But on January 11, 1876 when the boundaries of the new diocese were revealed, priests and laity expressed strong opposition. Domenec, who had wrestled with the idea for two years, exercised poor judgment by keeping his plans secret. To his way of thinking, the delay and secrecy were proper. However, the boundaries were unnatural and out of

Bishop John Tuigg

harmony with all geographical charts. The decision was immature, impolitic, and the cause of real financial injury.

THE DIOCESE OF ALLEGHENY

In 1864, Domenec evaluated the financial situation of the Diocese and reorganized his chancery staff. He spoke in glowing terms about his chancellor and secretary, Father John Hickey, to whom he handed over the supervision of all financial affairs. This assignment would eventually cause much anxiety and many problems for Bp. Tuigg.

John Hickey was born in Kilkenny, Ireland, on November 11, 1830. His uncle, Fr. Joseph Cody, was a priest of the Pittsburgh diocese. Sponsored by his uncle, John Hickey came to Pittsburgh in 1846 and was enrolled in St. Vincent College. He later attended Mt. St. Mary College and obtained a Master of Arts degree. Hickey was ordained by Bp. O'Connor on August 15, 1858. His first assignment was St. Patrick Church in Pittsburgh. Afterwards, Fr. Hickey taught at Mt. St. Mary Seminary and St. Michael Seminary, then located at Glenwood in the Hazelwood area.

In August 1862, when Fr. Richard Phelan was visiting in Ireland, Hickey substituted at St. Mary Church, Freeport. During his stay in Freeport, a diphtheria epidemic broke out. Parishioners in Freeport, Kittanning and Natrona were victims. Hickey responded to the crisis with a real missionary zeal and great strength of character.

While in Freeport he encouraged a young man, Andrew A. Lambing — the future priest and diocesan historian — in his priestly vocation. The life-long friendship between Hickey and Lambing dated from that time.

On January 6, 1863, Fr. John Hickey was appointed rector of St. Paul Cathedral. He had an affable and persuasive disposition. In many ways he was an excellent diplomat. Monsignor Lambing put it this way: Hickey "took well to people, and he had the dangerous gift of being able to borrow money."[1]

Fr. Hickey's talents and gifts gained him a great popularity, and his accomplishments were many. A gifted speaker, he could persuade almost any audience to agree with his plans and projects. As rector of

Monsignor Andrew A. Lambing, an eminent diocesan historian, was directed toward his studies for the priesthood during Bishop Tuigg's tenure.

the cathedral, he convinced the church committee that the debt had been reduced when he was paying only the interest on the loan.

When there was a dire need for a larger orphanage, Hickey initiated the purchase of land on Tannehill Street in the Hill District of Pittsburgh. A new orphanage was built on that site and dedicated in December of 1867 — just one year after the land purchase.

In 1868, and again in 1869, contrary to Bp. Domenec's expressed wishes, Hickey ordered the completion of the main towers of St. Paul Cathedral. As justification for ignoring the bishop's wishes concerning the towers, and later the cathedral rectory, he cited his apparent success as a fundraiser. Fr. Hickey is quoted as saying: "I was here before him [Bp. Domenec] and I will be here after him."[2]

In 1872, Fr. Hickey called a meeting of parishioners during which he insisted that the rectory (which had been damaged by fire on November 3, 1859) was not worthy of the Diocese or of the bishop, and he proposed plans for what some considered an elaborate residence. Bp. Domenec, present at the meeting, firmly rejected the plan and stated that he would not live in such a "palace."[3] The bishop left the meeting, but Hickey, undaunted, continued the meeting and received the parishioners' approval.

The fascinating power that Hickey had over the laity was even stronger when it came to his dealings with Bp. Domenec. Fr. Hickey's hold on the bishop was maintained and fostered by flattery, outright disobedience, and self-promotion. Bp. Domenec was concerned about Hickey's actions but timid in dealing with him. The debts on the orphanage, cathedral towers, and the rectory were so great that the combined interest was greater than the original estimated cost of their construction. The debt was beyond management.

On November 5, 1875, Bp. Domenec left Pittsburgh for Rome. He left quietly, telling no one the reason for his trip. He named Fr. Hickey as administrator of the Diocese during his absence.

Two months later, on January 16, 1876, Domenec was appointed the first bishop of the new Allegheny Diocese. On March 19, 1876, Fr. John Tuigg, the pastor of St. John Church, Altoona, was ordained by Archbishop James Wood of Philadelphia, in St. Paul Cathedral, as the third bishop of Pittsburgh.

On the afternoon of Tuigg's ordination, the entire entourage crossed the Allegheny River for Domenec's installation in St. Peter Cathedral, Allegheny City.

The division of the Diocese was not as sudden as Domenec's secrecy and actions made it appear. Bp. Domenec had been contemplating and working on the division since 1874. His original proposal suggested a north-south boundary, with the bishop's office in Altoona or Johnstown. Bp. Tobias Mullen of Erie, who had been pastor of St. Peter Church, Allegheny City, and vicar-general of the Pittsburgh Diocese, convinced Domenec to work for a diocese with its central offices in Allegheny City.

While in Rome, Domenec made frequent visits to the Congregation for the Propagation of the Faith in order to present what, to his mind, was the best division of the Diocese of Pittsburgh. Rome accepted his recommendations. The Diocese of Allegheny would comprise 6,530 square miles in 8 and 1/4 counties. The Diocese of Pittsburgh would comprise 4,784 square miles in 6 and 3/4 counties.

Domenec's secretive methods caused confusion and conflict. When the new and very irregular boundaries were announced, clergy and laity complained bitterly. The inequity of the division placed indebted parishes and institutions within the Pittsburgh Diocese, while those with better resources were all situated in the new diocese.

Clashes over assets and liabilities caused friction between Bishops Domenec and Tuigg. Trouble began when Tuigg refused to endorse notes for loans contracted during Domenec's tenure. Bp. Domenec, in turn, refused to transfer property deeds to Tuigg. A long-time friendship was disturbed, and much of the blame can be placed on the activities of Fr. John Hickey.

For 12 years, Domenec had placed complete confidence in Hickey's management of financial matters. As a result, the bishop was totally ignorant of the fiscal status of the Diocese of Pittsburgh, and Bp. Tuigg was unable to obtain a clear picture of the financial situation. Auditors reported to Tuigg a discrepancy of about $100,000 between receipts and disbursements. Bp. Tuigg contended that, despite Fr. Hickey's role, it was Bp. Domenec who was ultimately responsible for all financial matters and transactions during his administration.

Because of the enormity of the missing funds, Tuigg insisted that the matter be investigated by Rome. Domenec favored a local inquiry. In the meantime, an interim audit by Abp. Wood of Philadelphia failed to clarify the financial mess.

Determined to bring the situation to a conclusion, Bp. Tuigg sent Frs. Ferdinand Kittell and John Holland to Rome. In January 1877, these priests presented Tuigg's position to the Congregation for the Propagation of the Faith. Later, Domenec was summoned to Rome.

While the explanations presented by Kittell and Holland had been orderly, logical and well-documented, Bp. Domenec's presentation to the Vatican officials was seriously flawed. His response to the congregation's questions were emotional, repetitious and incomplete. It was a sad scene, and even Kittell and Holland empathized with Bp. Domenec.[4]

Rome's solution was fourfold: Domenec should resign and await another assignment. The Allegheny Diocese was to be reunited to the Diocese of Pittsburgh and governed by Pittsburgh's bishop.

Bp. Domenec complied with the Vatican decision and resigned on July 29, 1877. On his return to the United States, he stopped off in his native Spain. On December 30, 1877, he became seriously ill. A week later, on January 7, he died. The Archbishop of Tarragona presided at Domenec's funeral and burial. The second bishop of Pittsburgh — and the first and only bishop of the Allegheny Diocese — was buried in the Cathedral of Tarragona, Spain.

Pittsburgh newspapers raised some questions concerning Domenec's death. The *Commercial Gazette* insinuated that the bishop was not dead but that he was imprisoned in Rome because he had embarrassed the Vatican. The Archbishop of Tarragona and the American Consul at Barcelona testified to the normal circumstances of Domenec's death.[5]

TUIGG VS. HICKEY

As has already been noted, Fr. John Hickey played a central role in the problems between Bishops Domenec and Tuigg. Bp. Domenec's death and the unification of the Allegheny Diocese with the Diocese of Pittsburgh brought about a partial settlement of the difficulties. However, since Hickey had exercised complete financial control of the Diocese from 1864–1876, accusations of dishonesty began to surface. Tuigg asserted that "defalcation" had occurred and he would personally assume responsibility for all financial matters of the Diocese.[6]

On October 7, 1876, Hickey was removed as rector of the cathedral. He requested an assignment to another parish or permission to join another diocese. Tuigg, noted for severity, denied both of Hickey's requests and assigned him to the orphanage. At the orphanage, Hickey was provided food and lodging, but was not to receive a diocesan salary.

Fr. Hickey refused the assignment and retired to his family's home in Butler County. Tuigg's action, and Hickey's isolation, were resented by the priest's many friends. The Irish clergy, especially, saw it as a sad contest between a seemingly autocratic bishop and one of his priests.

Problems over Bp. Domenec's last will and testament added to the conflict. Hickey was one of the executors, but he refused to cooperate in some of the arrangements for the settlement of the will.

Fr. Hickey requested that a committee of priests be appointed to examine his responsibility for the discrepancies in financial reports on the status of the Diocese. After several months, this committee rendered a verdict in favor of Fr. Hickey. The bishop then appealed their decision to Rome. Tuigg and Hickey were summoned to the Vatican. On December 10, 1881, the Congregation for the Propagation of the Faith — after hearing both men — rendered its decision. While conceding that Hickey was a poor bookkeeper, the congregation found him innocent of any fraud or fraudulent intent. Fr. Hickey was to be allowed to accept a rural parish with the proviso that he be promoted to the next vacant parish in the city. Rome did stipulate, however, that Hickey could not return to St. Paul Cathedral.

Surprisingly, Tuigg did not see this decision as a defeat. The bishop appreciated the opportunity to present the case as he saw and understood it. Writing to Fr. Phelan, Tuigg said: "I am very glad that I came to Rome for now Rome has seen and learned how busybodies act and write."[7]

On March 19, 1881 — after declining two parishes — Fr. John

Hickey accepted the appointment of St. Thomas Parish in Braddock, where he remained for the next 23 years. This cultured and learned priest soon attracted the attention of Charles M. Schwab and Andrew Carnegie who gave him much support for St. Thomas Church.

One month after his 74th birthday, December 12, 1904, Fr. Hickey died. He is buried in the cemetery of St. John's Church at Coylesville.

FURTHER DIFFICULTIES FOR TUIGG

When the announcement had been made that Fr. John Tuigg was to become the third bishop of Pittsburgh, he received a letter from Bp. Patrick M. Lynch of Charleston, South Carolina. Bp. Lynch wrote: "I pray, since all mitres have thorns inside, and you no more than the rest of us can escape them, that in your case they may be softer than usual." Lynch's prayers, prophetic as to the thorns, were not answered for the third bishop of Pittsburgh.[8]

A series of serious problems confronted Bp. Tuigg during most of his ministry. On November 19, 1879, in a letter to Abp. Wood, Tuigg wrote:

> From the hour of my consecration up to this, I have, Most Reverend Archbishop, tried to be as conscientious as I could not only in my official, but private life, and notwithstanding this, my life is a martyrdom of trial. May God's will be done.[9]

Bp. Tuigg was a man of unbounded vigor and determination. Sometimes his manner was cold and harsh, but he always did what he thought best for the Diocese. There were times when his precipitious and imprudent actions aggravated complicated situations. He had a strong will, and he was not very flexible. Fr. Ferdinand Kittell left this evaluation: "Bishop Tuigg is, and always was, a thoroughly good man — governed in everything he did by the purest and best motives, but he committed many blunders under which we are still laboring."[10]

IRISH DISCONTENT

Bp. Tuigg created difficulties for himself and others by his treatment of Irish priests and laity. Three Irish organizations, The Ancient Order of Hibernians, the Molly Maguires (a secret society of coal miners who were not adverse to terroristic tactics when convinced that they were victims of unfair hiring practices), and The Emerald Benevolent Associations, were suspected and disapproved by many of the Irish bishops. Bp. Tobias Mullen of Erie, who had great influence on Bp. Tuigg, was one of these suspicious Irish bishops. Tuigg himself was strongly opposed to secret societies, and these three groups seemed to fit that classification.

Serious conflicts with two Irish priests, Fr. James Treacy and Fr. Patrick Sheehan, added to Bp. Tuigg's problems with his countrymen.

In 1874, Fr. Treacy had started, with Bp. Domenec's permission, a weekly Catholic newspaper. Treacy's paper, *The Hibernian* — later called *The Catholic Journal* — was in direct competition with the *Pittsburgh Catholic*. For whatever reason, Tuigg saw Treacy's paper as the organ of secret societies and, on December 9, 1876, forced it to suspend publication.

Fr. Treacy was also a problem for Bp. Tuigg on another score. Treacy — who had succeeded Tuigg as pastor of St. Brigid Church in the Hill district — was named an honorary chaplain to the Emerald Benevolent Association. Tuigg considered Treacy's acceptance of the appointment to be a personal affront. In April of 1877 he demanded that Fr. Treacy resign from the chaplaincy.

Tuigg's objection to *The Catholic Journal* and the chaplaincy of The Emerald Benevolent Association were seen by Fr. Treacy as unjust; and he requested permission to go to another diocese. Treacy left Pittsburgh and went on to minister as a priest in Chicago and Philadelphia. When his health began to fail, Fr. Treacy returned to the Diocese and lived with his brother, John P. Treacy, M.D. He died on November 8, 1898. His funeral Mass was celebrated in St. Brigid Church, the parish he had served for 23 years. He is buried in St. Mary Cemetery in Lawrenceville.

The situation with Fr. Sheehan came to a head when Sheehan

approached Bp. Tuigg, shortly after his installation, for an appointment as pastor of a parish. Fr. Sheehan had been away from the Diocese of Pittsburgh for about ten years. Originally he had been granted leave because of ill health, but for years he was absent without official permission. When he was refused a pastorate, Fr. Sheehan instituted a civil suit against Tuigg.

With ethnic loyalty, many Irish priests adopted the side of Fr. Sheehan. In the archives of the Diocese of Pittsburgh, there is a series of letters from Fr. William A. Nolan excoriating the bishop for persecuting Fr. Sheehan. But the last of Fr. Nolan's letters to Bp. Tuigg on this subject is a fervent apology for his previous letters; Fr. Sheehan's conduct indicated that the bishop had pursued the proper course in dealing with him.[11]

THE RAILROAD RIOT

In Stefan Lorant's book, *Pittsburgh, The Story of an American City*, there is a picture of Bp. Tuigg administering to victims of the riot that erupted during the Railroad Strike of 1877. This picture epitomizes the ministry of a much maligned bishop who served in troublesome times. Abp. Canevin described Tuigg's activities at the time of the riot as "heroic."[12]

As pastor of St. John Church, Altoona, Fr. Tuigg had been on friendly terms with the officials of the Pennsylvania Railroad — Altoona's primary employer. Since even church contributions were deducted from the railroad workers' pay, Fr. Tuigg did not have to plead for financial support from his parishioners.

The effects of the Panic of '73 were widespread. The Pennsylvania Railroad experienced a decline in income. In July 1877, in an effort to economize, the railroad reduced the employees' pay and planned to double the size of the freight trains by introducing "double enders." This meant that, in practice, two freight trains would be joined and operated by a single crew.

The first scheduled double-ender was to leave Pittsburgh on Thursday, July 19, but the assigned crew failed to report for work. The workers united and transportation came to a halt. Anticipating trouble, the railroad company summoned the Pennsylvania National Guard to protect their property.

People of the neighborhood were sympathetic with the workers. The Pittsburgh members of the National Guard fraternized with the strikers. The Railroad Company summoned 600 militiamen from Philadelphia. These additional troops aggravated and exasperated the strikers, who by this time were joined by a crowd anxious to vandalize property and buildings. When militiamen fired into the mob, a widespread riot developed.

Bp. Tuigg had made an attempt to avoid any confrontation. He had headed a delegation of citizens in an endeavor to urge the strikers to desist from any violence. This effort was not successful. Stefan Lorant writes: "As Bishop Tuigg walked the streets and prayed for the dying militiamen and workers, Pittsburgh was in the grip of a mob."[13]

Being unable to prevent the violence was a severe blow to Bp. Tuigg. He and Fr. Thomas Devlin were truly heroic in their ministrations during this turmoil.

Despite popular support for the railroad workers, the strike did not succeed. Twenty-five people had been killed, and $5 million damage was incurred. The strikers went back to work without having won any of the objectives for which they were striking.

The thorns predicted by Bp. Lynch never softened for Bp. Tuigg. In his tenure as the Bishop of Pittsburgh, he did make blunders. However, the number and variety of problems and personalities that confronted him precluded a perfect administration. He was challenged to bring order out of chaos, and to place the diocesan finances on a firm foundation.

Bp. Tuigg combined the qualities of firmness and gentleness to a degree rarely found in the same individual. He was strong and unyielding when he was confident of the justice and propriety of any position he held, but he was at the same time kind and courteous to those who held different opinions. Abp. Canevin expressed his regard for Bp. Tuigg in these words: "Proofs of his executive ability, his piety and his self-sacrificing zeal abound throughout the diocese over which God called him to rule, and which he left in better condition than it had known for years."[14]

LAST YEARS

In the last years of his life, Tuigg's once vigorous constitution was shattered by the burdens of his ministry. Not long after an 1881 visit to Rome, he contracted heart disease. Two years later he suffered two strokes and was paralyzed.

Because of his physical condition, Bp. Tuigg appointed Fr. Richard Phelan as vicar-general of the Diocese. In 1885, Phelan was ordained coadjutor bishop of Pittsburgh. With Phelan in place, Tuigg retired to Altoona where he died on December 7, 1889. He is buried in the cemetery of St. John's Church, Altoona.[15]

Bishop Richard Phelan

Seven

Richard Phelan
1889–1904
Fourth Bishop of Pittsburgh

"The administration of Bishop Phelan was a remarkably successful one. He was a man of prudent zeal and extraordinary business abilities," said Archbishop J. F. Regis Canevin.[1]

The death of Bp. Tuigg on December 7, 1889 marked a transition from discord and division to a time of peace, harmony and discipline, in the Diocese of Pittsburgh. At his death, the administration of the Diocese passed to Bp. Richard Phelan, who had been coadjutor for more than four years.

Phelan was born in Sralee, near Ballyragget, in County Kilkenny, Ireland on January 1, 1828. He began his seminary studies at St. Kieran College in Kilkenny. When Bp. Michael O'Connor visited that college in search of priests for the Diocese of Pittsburgh, Phelan volunteered and came to America.

Once in Pittsburgh, Phelan continued his studies at St. Michael Seminary, which was then located in the Birmingham section of the city. In 1851, when St. Michael Seminary closed, he was sent to St. Mary Seminary, Baltimore, Maryland.

In 1853, Bp. Michael O'Connor was appointed the first bishop of the Erie Diocese. O'Connor took Phelan with him to Erie. When Bp. O'Connor was returned to Pittsburgh, Richard Phelan was sent on to

115

St. Peter Church, North Side, which served as the cathedral for the Diocese of Allegheny, was destroyed by fire in 1886, a year after Bishop Phelan was appointed coadjutor bishop of Pittsburgh.

St. Mary Seminary, Cleveland, Ohio, where he completed his formation. Bp. O'Connor ordained Phelan on May 4, 1854, in the chapel of the bishop's residence in Pittsburgh, because the cathedral had been destroyed by fire.

Father Phelan was immediately appointed pastor of St. Patrick Church, Cameron's Bottom, in Cambria County. Eight months later, in February, 1855, a cholera and smallpox epidemic broke out in the city of Pittsburgh. Phelan returned to Pittsburgh and assisted the cathedral priests with their ministry to the sick. After the epidemic he returned to Cameron's Bottom, but within a year he was assigned to Pittsburgh and the cathedral church.

Pastors assigned to the churches in the Allegheny River Valley were experiencing difficulty with some of the parishioners, and their tenures were very short. In September 1858, Bp. O'Connor informed Phelan that he was sending him to Freeport. Fr. Phelan is said to have asked the bishop when he should report to his new assignment. "Tomorrow, Sir," was the bishop's reply.[2]

At Freeport Fr. Phelan was able to settle the problem in very short order, and for the next ten years he ministered (with perseverance and vigor) to St. Mary Parish and its numerous mission stations.

When Fr. Tobias Mullen left St. Peter Church, Allegheny, to become the third bishop of Erie, Phelan was appointed on July 21, 1868, by Bp. Domenec, to the rectorship of St. Peter's, then located on Anderson Street.

The location and the site of St. Peter Church was a disadvantage to the expanding parish. Phelan, with keen business tact, selected a new location near West Park, at Ohio Street and Sherman Avenue. Construction of a large stone church was soon begun, and the church was dedicated in 1874.

On March 19, 1876 — as a result of the division of the Diocese of Pittsburgh and the establishing of the Diocese of Allegheny — St. Peter Church became the cathedral of the Allegheny Diocese.

Phelan was appointed pastor of the cathedral church and served in that office until the reunification, August 3, 1877, of the Allegheny and Pittsburgh dioceses.

Phelan's performance of his duties convinced Bp. Tuigg of his sterling qualities and character. When Bp. Tuigg suffered a stroke in 1885, he selected Fr. Phelan as his assistant. On August 2, 1885, Phelan was ordained bishop by Abp. Patrick J. Ryan of Philadelphia, and assigned as coadjutor bishop of Pittsburgh.

Incapacitated by his stroke, Bp. Tuigg moved to Altoona. As coadjutor, Phelan had to make frequent, arduous and time-consuming trips to Altoona in order to confer with Bp. Tuigg about diocesan matters.

The last decade of the nineteenth century saw a great influx of people from Europe into the coal and steel industries and areas. This caused the Catholic population in the United States to triple in size, from $3\frac{1}{2}$ million to 12 million individuals. Of these newly arrived Catholics, about two million were from Germany and $1\frac{1}{2}$ million came from Ireland.

Alongside the newly arrived Irish and German Catholics, there came persons of many other nationalities, languages and customs. Their presence obliged the bishops to provide clergy, churches, schools and hospitals to meet the needs of the ever-growing and divergent Catholic population. The Diocese of Pittsburgh received a very large number of these immigrants. Almost every area of the Diocese was affected by their presence and spiritual needs. Bp. Phelan, himself, responded to their presence and needs by being sensitive to them and seeking out clergy to assist them.

THE CHURCH AND LABOR

The Knights of Labor, organized in Philadelphia in 1869, represents the first successful attempt to unite workers. Many bishops, convinced that the Knights of Labor was a secret society, were uncertain about both the organization and its members. Cardinal Elezear Tascheceau, bishop of Quebec, condemned the group, and had great influence on many of the bishops in the United States.

Cardinal James Gibbons and Bp. John Ireland, however, gave their full backing to both the labor movement and the Knights of Labor. Gibbons worked hard to insure that the Knights of Labor were not condemned by Rome. In 1887, Pope Leo XIII — who four years later was to issue the important encyclical *Rerum Novarum* — reversed Cardinal Tascheceau's condemnation of the Knight of Labor.[3]

THE SALE OF ST. PAUL CATHEDRAL

> Only those who have been associated with the cathedral for many years can appreciate the feelings of the older Catholics toward the beautiful and majestic Gothic structure, begun in hope and faith by Bishop O'Connor and his devoted band of co-workers fifty years ago.[4]

These words by John J. Benitz, editor of the memorial edition of the *Saint Paul's Cathedral Record* of May 10, 1903, begin an article on the sale of the Cathedral, which was located at Fifth Avenue and Grant Street in what had become the commercial center of the city. This final issue of the parish magazine reviewed the history of the Cathedral and the reasons why the venerable building had to be sold. The population of the parish had undergone drastic change as thousands moved from the central city to the suburbs. Since 1861, the income of the Cathedral had not been sufficient to meet the expenses of the parish and the payment of five percent on the debt.

Bp. Phelan was well aware of the situation and the crisis. However, it took him ten years to conclude that the sale of the Cathedral was a prudent and safe course of action.

As word circulated that the bishop was considering the sale, various offers were made for the property. These offers ranged from $750,000 to Henry Clay Frick's $1,325,000. When permission to sell the property was obtained from Rome, Frick's offer was accepted.

Before the sale was completed, a town-hall meeting of members of the cathedral congregation was convoked for April 2, 1901. Many persons who did not belong to the Cathedral attended this meeting and the variety of discussions prevented conclusive decisions.

A second meeting was called for April 9. This time only registered parishioners were invited to attend. The vote was 99 in favor and 68 opposed to the sale of the Cathedral. However, one person in attendance asked that the vote be unanimous, and all agreed with that decision.

Having obtained the approval of the laity, Bp. Phelan then asked the Court of Common Pleas to conduct a hearing on the matter. On May

24, 1901, the date assigned for the hearing, only two dissenters appeared in court. The court approved the sale of the Cathedral. On September 20, 1901 the deed to the cathedral property was transferred to Henry Clay Frick.[5]

During the next two years, the Church of the Epiphany was erected in the lower Hill District at Centre Avenue and Epiphany Street. Solemnly dedicated on August 20, 1903, Epiphany Church served the Catholic people who still remained in the territory of the Cathedral, and it was the pro-cathedral and residence of the bishop until the new cathedral at Fifth Avenue and Craig Street in the Oakland district was dedicated on October 24, 1906.[6]

After a third "lowering of the streets" by the city, the Union Trust Building was erected on the site of the cathedral at Fifth Avenue and Grant Street.

THE DIOCESE OF ALTOONA

In October of 1899, the bishops of the Province of Pennsylvania met in Philadelphia to consider a division of the Pittsburgh Diocese. Because of the Diocese's constant and continual growth, it was agreed that Bp. Phelan should be relieved of such a large responsibility. The bishops thought that Altoona might be a good site for a new diocese, and conveyed their opinion to Rome. But Rome failed to respond to their suggestion. The bishops reconvened on February 26, 1901, and re-presented their suggestion. Three months later, May 31, 1901, the Diocese of Altoona was established. Fr. Eugene A. Garvey of Scranton was selected as Altoona's first bishop. He was ordained in St. Peter Cathedral in Scranton on September 8, 1901, and took possession of his new diocese on September 28.[7]

The counties of Bedford, Blair, Cambria, Huntingdon and Somerset were transferred to the Diocese of Altoona.

DIOCESAN SYNODS

To foster a deeper religious life in the Diocese, Bp. Phelan convoked four diocesan synods.

Following the sale of St. Paul Cathedral in downtown Pittsburgh in 1901, Epiphany Church served as the pro-cathedral for the Diocese until the new St. Paul's was completed in Oakland in 1906.

The first synod was held February 7–9, 1893. A highlight of this synod was that it established an official Catholic school board.[8]

To promote clear and logical exposition of divine truth on this continent, religious schools were necessary. That is how it was until Horace Mann succeeded in replacing the religious schools of New England with his adaptation of Swiss and Prussian methods of education. This philosophy holds that education should deal only with practical aspects of life. Religion was excluded and had no influence on the curriculum.

This transition disturbed the American hierarchy. The Councils of Baltimore urged that schools be established in connection with all Catholic churches.

The clergy of the Diocese of Pittsburgh were strong in their belief that Catholic education affected the whole person by instructing students in the ways of God as well as in the ways of the world. To insure that their schools could maintain a high level of education, they established the Diocesan School Board to establish and supervise acceptable norms.

Diocesan synods of April 15,1896 and November 9, 1899 dealt with routine matters, but the synod of October 30, 1902 established the Pittsburgh Apostolate and a Commission on Sacred Music.

The Pittsburgh Apostolate was a band of diocesan priests dedicated to explaining the Catholic faith to separated brethren and to conducting revival missions in Catholic parishes in remote areas.

The Commission on Sacred Music was appointed to regulate and supervise the music to be sung in the churches of the Diocese. The Commission was to bring the diocesan churches into compliance with the ideals promulgated by Pope Pius X on November 22, 1903 in his *Motu Proprio* on church music.

ST. JOSEPH PROTECTORY

Two months after Bp. Phelan's first synod, on April 19, 1893, he wrote a letter to the priests of the Diocese describing the need of an institution that would serve as a protectory for working boys who were homeless. Many of these would be youth that had completed their stay at St. Paul Orphanage. He outlined plans for "a city home for industrious boys" that would be a memorial of the Golden Jubilee of the Foundation of the Diocese of Pittsburgh.

The managers of St. Paul Orphanage donated a site adjoining their Tannehill property. Construction began immediately and the building was under roof on November 2, 1893. It was dedicated on May 5, 1895, the feast of the Patronage of St. Joseph and the memorial building was named St. Joseph Protectory.

Printing, the first trade offered to the boys in 1896, was the staple occupation as long as the Protectory existed. In 1899, a second building was erected to serve as a workshop for the training in various trades.

Franciscan Brothers were the first supervisors of the Protectory, but they served only a short time. Brothers of Our Lady of Lourdes also directed the institution for a brief interval. They were succeeded by diocesan clergy, who managed the Protectory until it was closed in 1955.

ST. PAUL ORPHANAGE

St. Paul Orphan Asylum was started in 1838 by Fr. John O'Reilly. The Sisters of Charity staffed the orphanage until they were succeeded by Sisters of Mercy in 1845.

As the number of orphans continued to increase, the need for larger space was a constant problem. From the original quarters in the sister's convent to the former seminary on the South Side of the city, the orphans had been transferred to a large building on Tannehill Street in the Hill District in 1867. By the turn of the century, this building was inadequate to house the orphans.

On May 27, 1900, Bp. Phelan laid the cornerstone for a new building on a 17-acre plot outside the city at Idlewood, near Crafton. The planned capacity of this new orphanage was 1,200 children. For the next 60 years, St. Paul Orphanage was home for thousands of homeless children.

The Tannehill Street building became the residence of the St. Rita Home for Infants in June 1917, and was utilized as such until 1935. Later it became the St. Joseph House of Hospitality.

LAST YEARS

When Bp. Phelan neared the fiftieth anniversary of his ordination to the priesthood, he was given a coadjutor bishop, Fr. J. F. Regis Canevin. After the ordination of Bp. Canevin on February 24, 1903, Bp. Phelan retired to the new St. Paul Orphanage to spend his last years in peace and quiet.[9]

The only time Bp. Phelan left his residence at the orphanage was to celebrate his Golden Jubilee Mass in the Church of the Epiphany on May 4, 1904.

Seven months later, on October 20, 1904, Phelan died at the age of 77. He had been a priest for more than 50 years and a bishop for 20 years. He is buried in St. Mary Cemetery in Lawrenceville.

At his funeral Bp. Phelan was eulogized by Bp. P. J. Donahue of Wheeling, West Virginia, for "his kindness and charity, his simple unostentatious ways, his straightforward, honest candor void of political guile, his sterling qualities of mind and heart which made him a 'man among men.'"[10]

Bp. Canevin summarized the achievements of his predecessor in these words: "At his death Bishop Phelan was the head of a diocese which in organization, in personnel of its clergy, and its adequate equipment for the needs of the people, was second to none in the United States."[11]

Bishop Phelan (center with beard) marches in solemn procession at Epiphany Church during observance of the 50th anniversary of his ordination as a priest.

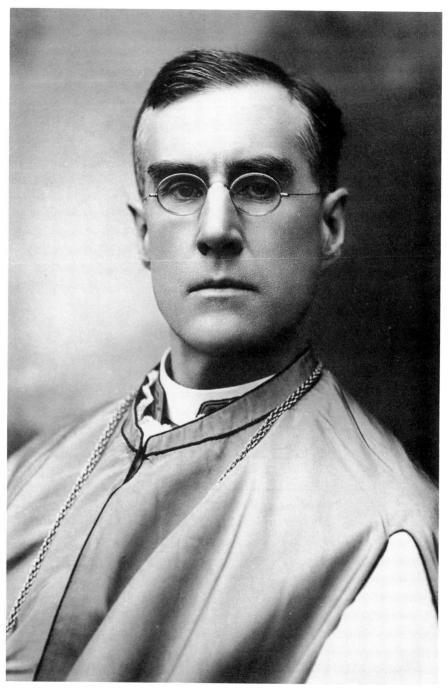

Bishop J. F. Regis Canevin

Eight

John Francis Regis Canevin
1904–1920
Fifth Bishop of Pittsburgh

> Bishop Canevin stilled the smouldering fires of religious prejudice. The hope, the fears, of more than one million metropolitan Pittsburgh people from every land under the sun, and of all creeds, were poured into his great soul, and came forth transmuted into peace, fraternity and civic pride. He gave his heart and his mind to the cause of humanity, following the example of Christ Himself.[1]

In these words, Cardinal James Gibbons, the archbishop of Baltimore summarized the character of the fifth bishop of the Diocese of Pittsburgh.

John Francis Regis Canevin was born at Beatty, Westmoreland County, PA on June 5, 1853. He received his primary education at St. Xavier Academy, a school conducted by the Sisters of Mercy, and completed his seminary studies at St. Vincent College and Seminary.

Regis Canevin was ordained by Bp. John Tuigg on June 4, 1879 in St. Paul Cathedral. Father Canevin's first assignment was to St. Mary Church, 46th Street, where he served as an assistant for two years. He spent the next five years as an assistant at St. Paul Cathedral.

In 1886 Canevin was appointed chaplain to St. Paul Orphanage and combined that ministry with duties at the state reform school at Morganza, at Western Penitentiary, and at the mission at Canonsburg.

127

His efforts at the penal institutions "won the unstinted praise and admiration of the denominational ministers who were brought into contact with him, and saw exemplified in his person the unselfish zeal and singleness of purpose of the Catholic priest. To the state officers this was a revelation, a new knowledge."[2]

In 1891 Canevin served — for a very brief period — as chancellor of the Diocese. His next assignment was to St. Philip Church, Crafton, as pastor.

Five years later he was appointed rector of St. Paul Cathedral. Rectory life, during this tenure, was described by a cathedral assistant as follows:

> We are not members of any religious order, nor are we bound by any special rules of life, and yet we think it would be difficult to find even in a monastery more exactness of discipline, more promptness to the call of duty than could be found among the priests of the Cathedral parish. If I were to lift the veil and reveal to you our domestic life, I would disclose to you a spirit of order, peace and brotherly concord which may be imitated by not surpassed, due to the kindly rule of our head, the reverend rector, Father Canevin.[3]

Bishop's Phelan's age and poor health required that he seek assistance, in the person of a coadjutor bishop, for the proper administration of the Diocese. There was community-wide interest and speculation on who would be selected. An August 25, 1902 article in *The Pittsburgh Dispatch* suggested that

> The splendid love of one Catholic father for another will probably result in the naming of Fr. J. Regis Canevin, rector of St. Paul's Cathedral, as coadjutor bishop to assist Rt. Rev. Richard Phelan, Bishop of Pittsburgh. The bishops of the Province of Philadelphia met yesterday at the episcopal residence on Grant Street and acted on the question of a coadjutor bishop, subject to the decision of the Holy see.
>
> To friends, Father Canevin has repeatedly declared that he hoped to escape the arduous labors of the coadjutor in the great Pittsburg district. On the other hand, Bishop Phelan has made no secret of the fact that he desired the rector of St. Paul's for his assistant.[4]

The Pittsburgh Gazette, on August 28, 1902 interviewed Francis P. Smith, LL.D., the veteran editor of the *Pittsburgh Catholic*. Mr. Smith summarized the qualities necessary for the office of coadjutor bishop.

> Whether the priest chosen for this sacred office be the choice of the irremovable rectors, or that of the bishops of the Province, so that he has all the qualifications required for this high office, the layman is perfectly satisfied. The diocese is great in its resources, spiritual and temporal. Its coadjutorship is no sinecure. The office will entail hard, unremitting labor. It demands a broadminded man to meet and keep in harmony its many nationalities. Racial proclivities need a wise head. The material life of the diocese is exacting and demands a man of administrative qualities.[5]

More than three months before Canevin's appointment, the *Pittsburgh Catholic* published a very laudatory article stating that:

> Father Canevin is adverse to praise, either privately expressed or more particularly in the newspapers. We should regard sacredly his innate modesty.
>
> As priest in charge of souls, that work speaks for itself wherever he was assigned. An idefatigable laborer in the vineyard, he never knew an idle moment. No matter how exacting the moment, he is prepared and ready. In the pulpit his manner is pleasing, his style attractive and his matter is always to the point, plain and instructive. His sermons are remembered for he is practical.
>
> In the confessional he is known as a wise spiritual counsellor. At the bed of sickness his presence is a consolation, while he hates the sin, he is tender and compassionate for the sinner. He realizes full well the infirmity of human nature. He is a rigid believer in total abstinence, but he is not fanatic in impressing his views. In devotion to the Sacred Heart he strives to lessen the evil of drink. His remedy is prayer through which comes the corresponding grace.
>
> Father Canevin is in manner reserved, yet thoroughly conversant with the canons of refined society, and is the pleasant gentleman with those he meets, either in the few moments of relaxation he permits himself, or in the duties at hand. He is a man of singleness of purpose, and comes directly to the point.[6]

While speculation on the selection of a coadjutor bishop was still rampant, an unusual accident presented another insight to the character of the popular candidate. *The Pittsburgh Post* of December 16, 1902 recorded an act of heroism by Fr. Canevin:

A notable instance of the modesty and whole-soul interestness of the coadjutor bishop nominee in this city occurred at the time of the Willey building disaster. A high wind blew down a partially completed structure on Diamond Alley and it fell upon the Weldin building and wrecked that one also. Imprisoned in the cellar of the Weldin building was a boy who could not be released on account of the danger of the rest of the building tumbling down.

Fr. Canevin was drawn to the scene and went down into the cellar at great risk of his life, learned from the boy that he was a Catholic and stayed down there until he had given him the last rites of the Church.

Later, for the rescue of this boy, at which Fr. Canevin assisted, Captain Peter Snyder had a gold medal voted for him by the City Council for his bravery.

Father Canevin almost got away unknown, but happened to be recognized by a couple of firemen.[7]

Speculation about the coadjutor bishop was ended with the announcement that Fr. Regis Canevin had been selected. Canevin was ordained by Archbishop Patrick J. Ryan of Philadelphia in St. Paul Cathedral on February 24, 1903.

Ten months later, when Bp. Phelan died on December 20, 1904, Canevin immediately became the fifth bishop of the Diocese of Pittsburgh. He was the first native son to be so honored.

BIGOTRY

Vestiges of the Know-Nothingism of the nineteenth century continued into the twentieth century. The genesis of the Ku Klux Klan and the Junior Order of American Mechanics provided a climate of bigotry as the number of Catholic immigrants settled in western Pennsylvania.

Bp. Canevin met attacks of bigotry calmly and in a spirit of Christian charity which treated and defeated intolerance with his equanimity and patience. With kindness and justice he was instrumental in healing festering wounds and fostering the relative calm of his own tenure as bishop.

Canevin was a serious student of religious prejudice and bigotry, and published articles in the *Pittsburgh Catholic* on the origin and motives of hostility towards Catholics. In one of his pamphlets, "Bigotry, the foe of liberty," he reviewed the history of the hatred and proscriptions of Catholics in colonial days. He indicated how European bigotry and persecution of Catholics were transplanted to this hemisphere.

On the political scene, Catholics were often accused of being disloyal to the United States because of professions of loyalty to the Holy See. One of the results of these accusations was a reluctance on the part of Catholics to take part in public affairs. Bp. Canevin advised Catholics to put aside this reluctance and seek public offices and public service. To strengthen his plea the bishop quoted John Ireland, the eloquent, energetic, progressive archbishop of St. Paul, Minnesota, who stated: "Should the particular case arise where it is plain that you are set aside solely because you are Catholics, then, in the name of Americanism, protest so loudly that never again will similar insult be offered to your American citizenship."[8]

RETREATS FOR THE LAITY

Until the time of Bp. Canevin's administration, there were no provisions in the Diocese for retreats for laypersons.

In 1911, Passionist nuns conducted a retreat for women in Our Lady of Sorrows convent on Churchview Avenue in the Carrick section of the city. In 1916 the sisters added facilities to their convent in order to accommodate retreatants.

The Holy Name Society assisted Canevin with his lay retreat project. Promoted by the Executive Committee of the Holy Name Society, a vigorous and substantial retreat movement for men was inaugurated. Summer retreats at St. Vincent College began.

In 1917, Thomas A. Coakley, pastor of Sacred Heart Church, and Joseph A. Beck, president of the Lay Retreat Committee, met with the Passionists at St. Paul Monastery to discuss the possibility of yearly weekend retreats.

The Passionists informed Coakley and Beck that they were willing to provide the spiritual assistance, but lacked the necessary facilities to accommodate the retreatants.

So, from March 4–11, 1918, Bp. Canevin authorized a diocesan campaign to raise funds for the Passionist monastery. With the cooperation of the Knights of Columbus, the Knights of St. George and the Holy Name Society, the campaign realized $60,000. Finally, in 1921, St. Paul Retreat House — adjacent to the monastery — was dedicated. And, Fr. Edwin Coyle, C.P., a native of Pittsburgh, was appointed the first retreat director.

CATHOLIC EDUCATION

As pastor of St. Paul Cathedral, Fr. Canevin was very interested in and involved with the parish school. When Canevin became bishop he determined that, in as much as possible, every parish ought to have a parochial school.

In 1904, Bp. Canevin appointed Fr. Thomas Devlin to be the superintendent of the diocesan schools. Devlin combined this work with his pastorate of Holy Cross Church in the Birmingham district of the South Side of Pittsburgh. Despite some opposition by pastors — who considered instructions from the superintendent as an infringement on their rights — Devlin did an extraordinary job. He standardized curricula, administration policies and the supervision of teachers.

After five years, Fr. Devlin resigned from this office. Canevin then appointed his secretary, Fr. Hugh C. Boyle, as full-time superintendent of schools. Boyle served until 1916 when he was assigned to the pastorate of St. Mary Magdalene Parish, Homestead.

Fr. Ralph L. Hayes succeeded Boyle and served from 1916–1925 when he was named pastor of St. Catherine Church, Beechview. Both later became bishops: Boyle served as bishop of Pittsburgh from 1921 until 1950; and Hayes as bishop of Helena, Montana, 1933–35, rector of the North American College in Rome, 1935–1940, and bishop of Davenport, Iowa 1944–1966.

Bp. Canevin's concern for Catholic education extended, of course, to both Duquesne University and St. Vincent College Seminary. As an especially loyal friend of Duquesne University, Canevin played an important role in Duquesne's 1920 financial campaign. Canevin Hall, on the campus of Duquesne University, was dedicated in 1922 and is a lasting memorial of his concern for Catholic education.

PUBLIC AND CIVIC AFFAIRS

At the start of World War I, when the loyalty of Catholics was again under attack, Bp. Canevin published a pamphlet entitled: "The Loyalty of Catholics." In this booklet he stressed how Catholics had always been loyal in peace and war. He skillfully defined the relationship between church and state, and declared that church and state ought to coexist in a spirit of mutual and friendly cooperation.

In 1917, in a talk at a public meeting in Syria Mosque in Oakland, Bp. Canevin said:

> When the government of a nation has declared that a state of war exists, war becomes the law of the land, and the law of the land demands obedience and loyalty of every subject. It is the duty of every citizen to defend his country's rights, maintain honor, protect from wrong, and aid it in securing a just and lasting peace.[9]

As a churchman, always seeking the well-being of religious endeavors, Canevin was also always the complete citizen. Many public and civic affairs could count on his endorsement, presence and even financial aid.

A good example of Bp. Canevin's influence and the participation in public and civic affairs is found in a letter, written at the time of the bishop's death by Edward A. Woods, president of the Tuberculosis League:

> Perhaps this letter should be addressed to Bishop Boyle. I did not know Archbishop Canevin's immediate family or whether he had any brothers or sisters, but you were so long his coadjutor and you knew him so well and I knew him so well that I want to express my appreciation of this wonderful character and I am therefore sending this letter to you to make what use of, if any, you wish.
>
> The privilege I had of being associated with so saintly a character as the archbishop was alone sufficient reward for anything I have ever done for the Tuberculosis League. I have known him most of my life, first when he was a priest, then a bishop and later archbishop. His presence at the meetings of our League has always been a benediction. His quiet attention to the business of the League was an inspiration to us all. At times he said scarcely a word during an entire meeting, but when he did

say anything his advice was always worthy of our most careful consideration. His exact knowledge of matters, far from what might be considered his field, was remarkable. Over and again matters came up, with which a priest would be presumed to be entirely unfamiliar, of which his knowledge — and precise knowledge — exceeded that of the entire board of directors of the League. His mind seemed to have pigeonholed almost any information that crossed it in such a way that he could recall it precisely at will.

Furthermore, the Archbishop's character ranks with that of the very few persons with whom it has been my privilege to come in contact even in the slightest way. He suggests to me such men as Dr. John G. Payton, one of the missionaries of our Church to the New Hebrides, and particularly Cardinal Mercier and Cardinal Gibbons, with a combination of impregnable character which would stand like the Rock of Gibraltar in a matter of principle, yet with a personal humility that approached almost more than any other I have every known the life of a Master he served so well and loved so much that he became like Him.

Few persons, if any, will be more keenly missed in the work of the Tuberculosis League, for his generous and unsparing efforts in the cause in which he was so deeply interested and his wise counsel were invaluable to us. It must be an inspiration to thousands of lives to have come in contact with so Christ-like a life.

Sincerely yours,
Edward A. Woods
President, Tuberculosis League[10]

CHILDREN WITH SPECIAL NEEDS

Immigration, poverty and recurring epidemics caused many children to be seriously ill. Deafness and blindness in children presented special problems, but there was no Catholic facility to care for them.

Monsignor Andrew A. Lambing was pastor of St. James Church, Wilkinsburg, which had the State School for the Deaf within its boundaries. Lambing and Canevin, concerned about both the spiritual and physical needs of these children, decided that a Catholic institution was required.

In 1907, three Sisters of Charity were sent to New England and

attended the Boston School for the Deaf in order to prepare themselves for work with children. The very next year, on September 7,
1908, the Pittsburgh School of Deaf Mutes, located on Troy Hill, was
opened.

Later, in the spring of 1911, Bp. Canevin opened DePaul Institute
for the Deaf. This institute, built in Brookline, eventually developed
into one of the finest oral schools for the deaf.[11] In the 1930s DePaul
Institute extended its care to children whose sight was impaired.

THE MISSIONARY CONFRATERNITY OF CHRISTIAN DOCTRINE

The steady arrival of new immigrants increased the Catholic population and brought new pastoral concerns. Most of the newcomers
worked in factories, on the railroad, or in coal mines. The spiritual care
of these immigrants many of whom, because of work, lived in sparsely
settled areas, was a special concern of Bp. Canevin.

In 1903, he launched The Pittsburgh Apostolate. Directed by Frs.
Edward P. Griffin and James L . Quinn, The Pittsburgh Apostolate
consisted of a small group of diocesan clergy whose special duty was
to travel to the outlying districts of the Diocese in order to preach
missions and organize catechism classes. To assist with religious
instruction, these priests founded the St. Ann Missionary Society,
which was composed of local people willing to teach.

When James Doyle and his family moved, in 1908, from St. John
the Baptist parish in Lawrenceville to the mining town of Cecil, they
were surprised to see that many of the local citizens were lax in matters
religious. James Doyle asked Anne Sweeney, director of catechism
classes at St. John the Baptist, to send some of her teachers to Cecil.
Two women, Mary Dunn and Anne Collins, came to Cecil on Sunday,
June 21, 1908, and began to teach catechism to the children of the
area. In a short time more teachers came to accommodate the growing
number of interested parents and children.[12]

Bp. Canevin heard about Doyle's efforts and realized that sending
trained teachers into the isolated areas might, in fact, be a solution to
providing religious instruction to people who lived in remote places.

The Mission Confraternity of Christian Doctrine was established in 1908 to provide religious instruction to people in remote areas of the Diocese. The second person to head this group was Father Daniel Lawless (center front) shown with other CCD leaders. They included Father Edward Heinrich (left front), Father Victor Majka (right front), and (rear, from left) Fathers Charles Thomas and Nicholas Biondi.

With Fr. Edward P. Griffin as coordinator, the Missionary. Confraternity of Christian Doctrine was established. Volunteer teachers attended bi-monthly classes and then traveled to the outlying areas for Sunday school.

In 1919, Fr. Daniel A. Lawless succeeded Fr. Griffin. When Lawless was appointed pastor of St. Mary of Mercy Church in downtown Pittsburgh, the headquarters of the Missionary Confraternity of Christian Doctrine was also located in that parish. Frs. Griffin and Lawless as well as the priests and laity who worked for the Confraternity labored with a real missionary zeal and enthusiasm. More than a fourth of the

The new St. Paul Cathedral in Oakland was dedicated in 1906.

parishes in the Diocese — beginning with Cecil in 1912 — can trace their origins to the efforts of the Missionary Confraternity. It was also the source of many vocations to the priesthood and religious life. The Missionary Confraternity of Christian Doctrine effort was a truly glorious chapter in diocesan history.

OTHER INSTITUTIONS

Bp. Canevin was responsible for many of the diocesan institutions that so greatly enhanced the growth of Catholicism in the first quarter of the twentieth century. In the 16 years he served as diocesan bishop, Canevin established an outstanding record. During those years, 134 new parishes were founded, and the bishop dedicated a parish or diocesan building for each month that he was Bishop of Pittsburgh.

The main accomplishment was the new St. Paul Cathedral, relocated from the downtown location at Fifth Avenue and Grant Street to Fifth Avenue and Craig Street in the Oakland area. The cornerstone of the Cathedral was laid by Bp. Canevin on September 4, 1904, and the edifice was dedicated on   October 24, 1906. The new cathedral was described by *The Pittsburgh Dispatch* as "a glorious testimonial to the devotion, sacrifices and generosity of nearly half-a-million fellows of the Catholic Faith."[13]

Canevin also initiated and fostered many other diocesan organizations. The Catholic Truth Society was founded in January 1899 to support literary endeavors. Canevin, himself, served as the first president and wrote many of the pamphlets published by the Catholic Truth Society.

The Catholic Club For Boys was formed in June 1901 at the Cathedral Lyceum then located at Fifth Avenue and Grant Street. The members of this club were young men who came directly under Canevin's influence. Years later, when they had made their mark in careers of education, finance, industry, and commerce, many of these would attribute their success to his guidance and influence.

The Holy Name Society, which had been introduced in the Diocese in August of 1884 by Fr. Thomas Devlin, pastor of Holy Cross Church on the South Side, had the approval of Bp. Canevin, and he directed

Bishop J. F. Regis Canevin (left) hosted Cardinal Mercier of Belgium during a visit in the early 1920s.

that the Holy Name Society be established in every parish throughout the Diocese.

Bp. Canevin endorsed and promoted the Knights of Columbus. In turn the Knights became the bishop's main financial assistance with many projects — especially the Missionary Confraternity of Christian Doctrine.

In 1910, a Conference of Catholic Charties was set up to coordinate diocesan charitable activities. This organization, founded by three attorneys — Hon. A B. Reid, John Marron, and Charles D. Gillespie — with the approval and supervision of Bp. Canevin, was one of the first diocesan central bureau of charities to be established in the United States.[14]

RESIGNATION

When Bp. Canevin began his ministry, the Catholic population under his care was 225,000. At his resignation in 1920 it had increased to 700,000 and was the second largest diocese in the United States. During the 18 years that he was a bishop — two years as coadjutor to Bp. Phelan and 16 years as bishop of Pittsburgh — the number of priests doubled and the number of religious women tripled.

Years of strenuous activity impaired Bp. Canevin's health. He resigned as Bishop of Pittsburgh on November 26, 1920.

At his retirement, in recognition of his accomplishments, he was given the title of archbishop. In retirement, he served as chaplain to the Felician Sisters at their convent near McKeesport. He continued to be interested in the progress of the Church and the Diocese.

Abp. Canevin died in Mercy Hospital on March 22, 1927. He was 74 years old. At his death, Sisters of Mercy — who had known him well — gathered his personal effects and set them aside to be preserved as relics of a man whom they and many others considered a saint. Canevin's funeral took place in St. Paul Cathedral on March 26, 1927. He is buried in St. Mary Cemetery, Lawrenceville.

Bishop Hugh C. Boyle

Nine

Hugh C. Boyle
1921–1950
Sixth Bishop of Pittsburgh

THE JOHNSTOWN FLOOD

On May 31, 1889, after a very heavy all-night rainfall, the old South Fork reservoir — which had been built to supply water for the Pennsylvania Canal, but later was a vacation resort for Pittsburgh industrialists — collapsed and released 65 million tons of water in the valleys of the South Fork and Little Conemaugh Rivers. The city of Johnstown was inundated, and much of it completely destroyed, in the famous Johnstown Flood. More than 2,200 people lost their lives in the catastrophe.[1]

At Saint Vincent College in Latrobe, 35 miles to the west, Hugh Boyle, a 15-year-old seminarian learned of the disaster and walked most of the way to Johnstown; only to discover that his father, four brothers and three sisters had been killed. Only his mother and baby brother Michael were miraculously saved. In the water, his mother's hair became entangled on a spike protruding from a log which kept her head above water until she was rescued at Lockport, 28 miles from Johnstown. The baby Michael slipped from the arms of one rescuer but fortunately was later rescued by another.[2]

After the catastrophe, Boyle returned to St. Vincent, continued his studies for the priesthood, and was ordained on July 2, 1898.

His first assignment was a three-week stint at St. Thomas Church in Ashville. On August 25, 1898 he was appointed as an assistant at St. Aloysius Church, Wilmerding, where he remained until January 25, 1903, when he was sent to St. Paul Cathedral and served as secretary to Bishop Canevin.

He remained at the cathedral — in its three locations: Fifth Avenue at Grant Street, Epiphany church and at the Fifth Avenue and Craig Street — until March 19, 1909, when at age 36 he was appointed the first full-time superintendent of schools. To prepare for this assignment Father Boyle attended the Catholic University of America for special studies in school administration.

In November of 1916, Boyle became pastor of St. Mary Magdalene parish, Homestead. In 1919, during his Homestead pastorate, steelworkers went on strike. Boyle distinguished himself in his care for and support of the strikers.

SIXTH BISHOP OF PITTSBURGH

As superintendent of schools and as pastor of St. Mary Magdalene Church, Fr. Boyle, who had a wonderful personality and a great sense of humor, was a very popular priest. He loved to walk and was kind and gracious to all whom he met.

When Bp. Canevin resigned, Fr. Boyle was the popular choice for the next bishop of Pittsburgh. It was, then, not unexpected when on June 16, 1921, Benedict XV named him as the sixth bishop of Pittsburgh. Boyle was ordained by Archbishop Canevin in St. Paul Cathedral on June 28, 1921.[3]

The priests of the Diocese expressed their approval in a congratulatory letter from the deanery of Fr. W. P. Dunlea. "Rarely has a bishop been named whose appointment has given more pleasure to his fellow priests than that of Bishop Boyle. Their approval is a compliment to him and to them. It shows that they recognized his ability and loyalty and that no selfish jealousies have a place in their heads."[4]

Tragedy almost marred Bp. Boyle's first public function. On July 3, 1921, Boyle blessed St. Anthony Village in Oakmont. After the

Bishop Boyle (right) stands outside St. Paul Cathedral following his 1921 ordination as bishop with Cardinal Dennis Dougherty of Philadelphia, principal celebrant at the ceremony.

liturgical ceremony, the bishop and Vittorio Rolandi Ricci, the Italian Ambassador to the United States, were seated on the speaker's platform. As Boyle began to speak, the platform collapsed. No one was injured, so the bishop and the ambassador continued the program at another location.[5]

Fr. James A. W. Reeves, in 1943, wrote of Bp. Boyle: "In the seminary he developed a fondness for beauty of thought and of idiom that mark his oral and written expression, and which have carved out a style that makes conversation bright and engaging even among persons whose interests and tastes vary."[6]

Bp. Boyle was a great conversationalist. On informal occasions he would introduce a topic which he had recently reviewed and thus control discussion.

Bp. Boyle's love for "the destitute little ones at the orphan's asylum" was shown every Christmas in the letters of petition that he himself wrote.[7] These letters were beautiful examples of his literary style, and were well received. In an effort to insure funds for the orphanage, Boyle decreed that all monies collected at the Masses celebrated on Christmas day were to be transferred to the St. Paul Orphan Asylum. The need, of course, was very great. During Boyle's time the orphanage had an average population of more that 1,000 children. The Christmas collection was the largest source of income for the care of the orphans.

THE EDUCATION CAMPAIGN

The story of Bp. Boyle's administration is filled with many services that he performed, and the projects in which he was interested, but his chief concern was Catholic education.

In a pastoral letter written on February 18, 1924, Boyle noted that there were 211 parish schools and 42 Catholic high schools in the Diocese. He stressed how this represented an enormous amount of sacrifice on the part of the Diocese. Eighty thousand children were receiving a thoroughly Catholic and American education from 1,200 teachers. The bishop lamented that another 54,000 Catholic children (40% of the total school population) were not receiving such an education and that almost one-half of the Catholic children were being sent into the world only partially equipped to live a Catholic life.

In particular, Boyle decried the small minority that could be accommodated in Catholic high schools. He averred that Catholics were not leaders in the professions and that their influence was not proportionate to their numbers. He advocated an increase in Catholic high schools, in the conviction that these would close the gap in the Catholic education system.

To achieve this goal, Boyle announced and outlined a diocesan-wide campaign to obtain funds for Catholic education in every parish, and especially to erect Catholic high schools in strategic districts of the Diocese. The bishop challenged 650,000 Catholics — amounting to

130,000 families — to raise $3,000,000 in a period of five years. A main goal of the campaign was to make it possible for the smallest and poorest parishes to enjoy the same educational advantages as the largest and best equipped parishes.

The education program was enthusiastically endorsed by parish committees throughout the Diocese.

The campaign was conducted from March 29 to April 7, 1924. At its conclusion, payments and pledges amounted to $5,000,000. Central Catholic High School in Oakland, and North Catholic High School on Troy Hill were the primary beneficiaries of the campaign.[8]

THE KNIGHTS OF COLUMBUS NORMAL SCHOOL

The Knights of Columbus Normal School was one of the most significant steps in affording Catholic school teachers professional qualifications. In 1920, the Pennsylvania Department of Education established the requirement that every teacher must have two years of normal school training beyond high school. Many of the sisters teaching in the Catholic schools lacked the formal education necessary for this certification.

Bp. Boyle and Fr. Ralph Hayes, Catholic schools superintendent, had to address the certification problem. The Knights of Columbus — with the professional assistance of Prof. Michael J. Relihan of Seton Hill College, later president of Mercyhurst College in Erie — helped resolve the problem by establishing a normal school for Catholic school teachers. Approved by the Department of Education in Harrisburg, the normal school opened in October of 1921 in the Knights of Columbus Hall on the North Side, with 225 students in attendance. As time went on, the original volunteer faculty of six gradually increased to 25. These volunteers were dedicated teachers instructing in 17 subject matters and preparing colleagues in the Catholic schools. Every Saturday morning during the school year, Catholic school teachers requiring certification attended these courses at the Knights of Columbus Hall. In summer, courses were held at Duquesne University, or at the motherhouses of the various religious communities.

In its first decade this normal school enabled more than 1,500 women religious to obtain certification. In 1925 the normal school was moved from the Knights of Columbus Hall to St. Peter School, North Side.

At St. Peter School, a model elementary school library — used as an extension of the normal school — was set up. The library prepared teachers for the administration of school libraries.[9]

In 1932 Bp. Boyle, at the request of the Commonwealth of Pennsylvania, designated Duquesne University, Mount Mercy (Carlow) College, and Seton Hill college as approved teacher-training centers for the Catholic schools of the Diocese. This designation superceded the Knights of Columbus Normal School and it was discontinued at that time, but its work made valuable contributions to the progress of Catholic education in the Diocese.

Throughout Bp. Boyle's administration the priests who succeeded him as superintendent of schools continued to introduce and foster improvements in the Catholic school system. Frs. Ralph L. Hayes (1916–1926), Paul E. Campbell (1926–1939), and Thomas J. Quigley (1939–1955) each built upon the accomplishments of their predecessors and realized excellent schools and supervising departments.

The idea of the *Christian Teacher* — as described by Pius XI in his 1929 encyclical on *The Christian Education of Youth* — was foremost in the goals of the diocesan schools department. In that encyclical, Pius XI had stated:

> Perfect schools are the result not so much of good methods as of good teachers, teachers who are thoroughly prepared and well-grounded in the matter they have to teach; who possess the intellectual and moral qualifications required by their important office; who cherish a pure and holy love for the youths confided to them, because they love Jesus Christ and His Church, of which these are the children of predilection, and who have therefore sincerely at heart the true good of family and country.[10]

When Bp. Boyle accepted the governance of the Diocese he was well aware of the task before him. At that time, 1921, the Diocese ranked ninth in Catholic population, had the largest number of churches and was fourth in the number of schools. The ethnic parishes of the Diocese used 17 different languages. Boyle's experience as superintendent of schools had taught him much about the extent and variety of the parishes. He knew that the Diocese was a polyglot area that would continue to evolve because of immigration.

In the years after World War I, the National Catholic War Council became the National Catholic Welfare Conference. Bp. Boyle enthusiastically entered into the work of the National Catholic Welfare Conference and served, for many years, on the executive board. In 1929 he was selected as chairman of the Department of Education. From 1930 to 1935 he chaired the Press Department and from 1937 to 1942 he headed the Legal Department.

While chairman of the Press Department, the bishop managed to extend the NCWC News Service to 21 countries. Lamenting that it was "painfully evident"[11] that few Latin American countries were members, he laid the groundwork for expansion in those countries.

From 1923 to 1943, Bp. Boyle served on the board of trustees of the Catholic University of America. He also served on the bishop's War and Emergency Relief Committee, and the Committee on Polish Relief.[12] From 1924 on, he maintained a life membership in the American Catholic Historical Society, Washington, DC.

CHURCH MUSIC

To foster and maintain good ecclesiastical music in the churches of the Diocese, Boyle invited Fr. Carlo Rossini to Pittsburgh. In 1923, Rossini arrived from Rome and took charge of diocesan music. He immediately set out and defined minimum standards for acceptability.

Seven years after his arrival, a Diocesan Music Commission was established. The commission stipulated the goals and minimum requirements expected of musicians. It recommended and proscribed hymns for church use and conducted classes for organists and choir directors. A Board of Examiners was appointed in 1931. All organists were subject to an examination of their competency. Weekly organ recitals in Synod Hall were part of the program of the Music Commission.[13]

The Music Commission published educational and informative articles in the *Pittsburgh Catholic*. It also distributed a blacklist of parishes not in compliance with the commission's regulations.

Bishop Boyle (right), who headed National Catholic Welfare Conference's Education Committee, is shown in 1935 with fellow committee members (from left) Archbishop John Cantwell of Los Angeles, Archbishop John T. McNicholas of Cincinnati and Bishop John F. Noll of Fort Wayne, Ind.

Father Carlo Rossini came to Pittsburgh from Rome in 1923 at Bishop Boyle's invitation to head up the diocesan music effort.

Fr. Rossini's methods were not always appreciated. He banned hymnals which had been popular and substituted a book featuring texts selected by him. However, Rossini's long-term governance of diocesan music programs did succeed in both fostering and maintaining a high level of musical excellence and competence in the Diocese.

AD LIMINA APOSTOLORUM

Every five years, all diocesan bishops are required to file a report with the Vatican on the spiritual and material condition of the diocese entrusted to their care. This personal visit to Rome, Vatican offices and the Pope himself is called the *Ad Limina*.

In 1925, Bp. Boyle went to Rome for his *Ad Limina* visit. This was the only visit that he ever made to the Vatican. There is no specific explanation for his subsequent actions, but apparently he was so disillusioned with his first visit that he never again returned. After 1925, the quinquennial reports for the Diocese were sent to Rome but Bp. Boyle stayed at home.

Boyle was an enigmatic person. In his younger years he was very popular with most priests and with the religious and laity who came to know him. In his final years, the bishop was very much changed and reclusive.

The office of bishop and its duties altered his relationship with even his closest friends. His priest friends shied away from him so as not to subject the bishop to any charges of favoritism. Clergy and laity seeking special favors — a practice which Boyle detested — were the only persons who sought appointments with him. Boyle gradually withdrew from appearing in public except for official and liturgical functions. An avid reader, afflicted with insomnia, the bishop's day was not a normal one. Sleepless nights resulted in late rising, private Masses in his private chapel, and diocesan affairs conducted in his private office at the bishop's house. Important papers and proposals would be brought to his attention by the diocesan chancellor and his personal secretary.

The day-to-day management of the Diocese devolved upon Fr. Peter C. Danner who was chancellor during much of Boyle's term. Danner was assisted in his work by Frs. Theodore Klimke and Edward Misklow. Frs. Jerome Hannan (later Bishop of Scranton) and Msgrs.

Andrew Pauley and Paul R. Coyle served as Boyle's personal secretaries and assisted in the administration of the Diocese.

For many years the chancery office was a three-man operation but death reduced it by one. The death of Fr. Theodore Klimke, on a Sunday morning in 1937, was shocking. Klimke, a beloved pastor of St. Mary Church, Pine Creek (Glenshaw), died in the sanctuary just as he was completing Mass. Overcome by illness at Communion time, Klimke sat in a chair as his parishioners knelt before him to receive the Eucharist. When the last communicant had received the Sacred Host, Fr. Klimke died. A priest was summoned from St. Mary Church, Sharpsburg, to anoint Fr. Klimke and to conclude the Mass.

After Fr. Klimke's death Fr. Edward Misklow took over Klimke's duties. Two years later, in 1939, Fr. Danner died and Misklow assumed Fr. Danner's duties also. Within two years, two chancery priests had died and Fr. Misklow (a workaholic) simply absorbed all their administrative duties.

A diocesan bishop is required to have a Board of Consultors with whom he must confer about some diocesan business. Bp. Boyle based his selection, for most of his consultors, on their ethnicity. The apparent leaders of the various nationalities were appointed consultors. As a consultor the priest was seen as a resource for and an advocate of his ethnic group.

Bp. Boyle's latter leadership style — mild and almost impersonal — produced a clergy with considerable personal initiative. The Diocese, its activities and organizations continued to thrive and develop.

Under the leadership of the dynamic Fr. James Delaney, the Diocesan Holy Name Society attained its zenith. Monthly Masses and meetings gave the men of each parish a feeling of religious solidarity. The Holy Name Society parades, discontinued because of anti-Catholic reaction, had an impressive successor.

Eucharistic Night celebrations (at Forbes Field in 1930, Pitt Stadium in 1936, and again at Forbes Field in 1941) were magnificent expressions of the faith of thousands of men and boys.

After Delaney's tragic death in a 1938 automobile accident, Fr. Alvin W. Forney continued Delaney's work. One of Boyle's last appointments, in 1949, was that of Fr. Paul Lackner as spiritual director of the Holy Name Society.

The famed Jesuit, Fr. Daniel Lord — a master in conveying Catholic teachings and ideals to young persons — was a great impetus to the vitality of the diocesan sodality of the Blessed Virgin. Archbishop Coleman Carroll and Msgr. Oliver Keefer were the sodality's spiritual moderators. Each year, Lord came to Pittsburgh for a meeting of the sodalists. So many young women would attend this annual meeting that the facilities of the William Penn Hotel were insufficient to accommodate them. Unfortunately, the sodality did not survive the post-World War II period.

THE CATHOLIC RADICAL ALLIANCE

In the late 1930s, during the Depression, the Catholic Radical Alliance was formed in Pittsburgh. An extension of the Catholic Worker philosophy and Dorothy Day's inspiration, the Catholic Radical Alliance emphasized the dignity of the individual person, worked for basic human rights and was especially concerned with politics and employment. In Pittsburgh, Msgrs. George Barry O'Toole and Carl Hensler were the Alliance's theorists and planners. Msgr. Charles Owen Rice was its spokesman and activist. It was Rice's task to apply, locally and practically, the ideals of The Catholic Radical Alliance. Msgr. Rice founded the St. Joseph House of Hospitality as a practical and tangible result of the Alliance. During the Depression it ministered to any unemployed and homeless men.

Another effect of the Alliance was the organization of labor unions for mine and steel workers. Three labor leaders, all members of Resurrection Parish, Philip Murray, Patrick Fagan and John J. Kane were prominent organizers of labor unions.

THE CATHOLIC EVIDENCE GUILD

In the early 1940s, a group of priests and laymen engaged in street preaching. At street corners, mainly in the Hill District, and on soap boxes, they preached Jesus Christ and His teachings to all who would listen. This great experience had — because of World War II — a short life. But while it lasted, it was most effective.

THE HOUSE OF MARY

The needs of poor persons living in the Hill District had been a topic of discussion for many years, but little was done to alleviate their situation. The Hill District problem had been studied by the Russell Sage Foundation and other research organizations. There was great need of spiritual and material assistance. The sisters at Roselia Hospital tried — in periods when free from their duties — to give some assistance. In 1944, Srs. Cyril Aaron and Angelica Little — both on the faculty of Seton Hill College — established the House of Mary on Webster Avenue. The sisters lived with the persons whom they hoped to serve. As their presence was accepted and their work progressed, the House of Mary staff increased.[14]

DIOCESAN FINANCES

Bp. Boyle was ever conscious and cautious concerning the diocesan financial situation. At a time of national financial depression the Diocese was expanding and Boyle sought every means to conserve diocesan and parish resources. He oversaw the consolidation of insurance coverage on church properties which resulted in reduced risk and premiums. Centralized buying of essentials, for parishes and institutions, through the Diocesan Purchasing Commission was also started during Boyle's tenure.

MILITARY CHAPLAINS

Pittsburgh and its industries always played a vital role in supplying war-time tools and weapons. The Diocese also contributed many of its sons and daughters to active service. It also made a great contribution to the welfare of service men and women by supplying many military chaplains who often rose to high ranks in the armed forces.

In *Among the Mescalero Apaches*, the biography of Fr. Albert Braun,

O.F.M., — an army chaplain in the First and Second World Wars — there is an item concerning a Pittsburgh priest. It records Fr. Herman C. Baumann's heroic acts, rescuing soldiers while stationed on Corregidor, and as a prisoner of the Japanese. On one occasion Baumann entered a burning building — through a window — to perform a rescue mission. His commanding officer, Lt. Col. Mitchell of the 9th Coast Artillery stated that he would recommend Fr. Baumann for the Congressional Medal of Honor. However, Colonel Mitchell was lost at sea while returning to the United States so the recommendation was never recorded.[15]

NATIONAL LEADERSHIP

At Bp. Boyle's installation on June 30, 1922, Cardinal Dennis Dougherty of Philadelphia noted that the bishop had been chosen because of his intellect, virtue and piety.[16] Boyle was popular with his brother bishops. At their annual meetings in Washington, many of the bishops sought out and waited for his summary of the subject being studied. He was an expert in giving a concise report and summary of a lengthy presentation. Bp. Boyle had a retiring nature, but when he presided at liturgical functions he rose to the occasion and inspired devotion and reverence.

NATIONAL AND LOCAL EVENTS

The years of Boyle's ministry (1921–1950) were turbulent times with unusual political and civil situations. Besides the Depression and World War II, the Diocese was affected by various local and national events.

In 1928, Alfred E. Smith — a Catholic, four-term governor of New York State — was defeated in the presidential election. The hectic and anti-Catholic campaign associated with Smith's efforts reawakened the problems of bigotry.

On July 23, 1931, a fire destroyed the Penn Avenue home of the Little Sisters of the Poor. Forty-two of the residents, aged and poor, died in this tragedy. Boyle and the entire diocese were shocked, and responded with spiritual and financial assistance.[17]

155

Father James Cox, pastor of St. Patrick's in the Strip District, led a group of unemployed to Washington in 1932 to demonstrate about the effects of the Depression.

A year later, January of 1932, Fr. James R. Cox, pastor of St. Patrick Church — known as the Shepherd of the Unemployed — led his Jubilee Army March to Washington in order to demonstrate about the effects of the Depression. Many of the unemployed had to live in Cox's Shanty Town in the Strip District of Pittsburgh. Later in the same year, Cox himself became the presidential candidate of the Jobless Party.[18]

During the Second World War, Boyle's help was often sought. He was a leader in supporting the buying of War Bonds, community fund endeavors and foreign relief programs.

At the 1941 dedication of the Catholic Worker School, Bp. Boyle declared that labor and the general public had been misled by those "whose economic philosophy is opposed to the fundamental rights of human dignity. The labor movement in this country is on the march. It needs to grow soundly."[19]

LAST YEARS

As Bp. Boyle grew older, the Diocese continued to expand. It had become the second largest diocese in the country. Only the Diocese of Brooklyn, New York, was larger. Pittsburgh was eighth in size among all the archdioceses and dioceses of the United States. Only two of all the ecclesiastical jurisdictions exceeded Pittsburgh in the number of parishes and elementary schools.

While other bishops helped with the administration of the Sacrament of Confirmation, the Diocese was too large and the duties were too numerous for a single bishop. Assistance came with the appointment of a coadjutor. On March 13, 1948, Rome appointed — without Boyle's request — Msgr. John F. Dearden, of Cleveland, Ohio, coadjutor to the bishop of Pittsburgh with the right of succession.

In August of 1949, Mr. and Mrs. David I. McCahill donated their Warwick Terrace home to the Diocese as a residence for the Bishop of Pittsburgh. Boyle visited the house but never lived in it.

Bp. Boyle died in Mercy Hospital on December 22, 1950. After a Pontifical Mass in St. Paul Cathedral on December 27, the bishop was buried in St. Mary Cemetery in Lawrenceville.

This 1940 view of St. Patrick Church in the Strip District shows the new church which was constructed after a fire destroyed its predecessor. The earlier church covered an entire block, including the open space in the left center of the photo.

Ten

John Dearden
1950–1959
Seventh Bishop of Pittsburgh

John Francis Dearden was born in Valley Falls, Rhode Island, on October 15, 1907. He began his elementary studies at Holy Trinity School in Central Falls, Rhode Island. When he was 11 years old, his father was promoted to be superintendent of a General Electric Corporation plant in Cleveland, Ohio. The family moved to Ohio and St. Philomena Parish in East Cleveland where he attended the parish school.

At the Cathedral Latin School in Cleveland, Dearden was taught by Father Edward A. Mooney, later cardinal archbishop of Detroit. He was graduated from the Cathedral Latin School in 1925. In the fall of the same year, he began formal studies for the priesthood at St. Mary Seminary, Cleveland. In 1929, he was sent to the North American College in Rome, Italy, and he studied theology at the Gregorian University.

Dearden was ordained a priest in Rome on December 8, 1932. After ordination he remained in Rome where he completed his studies and was awarded a doctorate in theology.

In 1934, John Dearden returned to the United States and was assigned as an assistant at St. Mary Parish in Painesville, Ohio. Three years later, he was appointed to the faculty of St. Mary Seminary,

Cardinal John Dearden

Bishop Dearden presides at 1950 funeral of his predecessor, Bishop Boyle. At far left is Father William Connare, who later became bishop of Greensburg.

Cleveland. In 1944, Archbishop Schrembs named him rector of the same seminary.

As rector, Dearden proved himself an able administrator and educator. His talents as the coordinator of many diocesan projects — which he directed with calm and a passive demeanor — earned him the nickname "Iron John," according to priests in Cleveland.

COADJUTOR TO BISHOP BOYLE

On March 13, 1948 at 41 years of age, Dearden was appointed coadjutor (with the right of succession) to Hugh C. Boyle, Bishop of Pittsburgh. John Dearden was ordained bishop in St. Agnes Church, Cleveland, on May 18, 1948.[1] He came to Pittsburgh in time to join the observance of Bishop Boyle's 50th anniversary of ordination, which was celebrated on June 21, 1948.

Bishop Dearden visits DePaul Institute, a school devoted to educating persons with hearing impairments.

Bp. Dearden resided at Mount Mercy — now Carlow — College. For the next two years he assisted Boyle and made a careful study of the Diocese.

SEVENTH BISHOP OF PITTSBURGH

Boyle died on December 22, 1950. Bp. Dearden succeeded him as the seventh bishop of Pittsburgh. His 18 months of study and observation provided him with information about and insights into his new ministry. Dearden was well aware that more services, churches and schools were needed to accommodate the growing and shifting population of southwestern Pennsylvania.[2]

In May of 1951 — five months after Bp. Dearden began his ministry — the four eastern counties of the Diocese (Westmoreland, Armstrong, Indiana and Fayette) were separated from Pittsburgh to form the Diocese of Greensburg. Bp. Hugh L. Lamb, who had been the administrator of the Archdiocese of Philadelphia, was appointed Greensburg's first bishop. Lamb did not, however, assume his responsibilities until January of 1952. So, from May 1951 until Bp. Lamb's arrival in Greensburg, Dearden had the responsibility of directing the Church in both Pittsburgh and Greensburg.[3]

Dearden's administrative abilities soon became evident as he set about to reorganize the Diocese of Pittsburgh. With priestly zeal and shrewd business acumen, he reviewed all aspects of diocesan life. He moved the chancery office from Oakland to the city; and saw 28 churches and 23 schools built during his nine years as bishop of Pittsburgh.

Additionally, many organizations already in existence were either renewed or terminated, and many new groups were soon formed. The Missionary Confraternity of Christian Doctrine was supplanted by the local version of the National Confraternity of Christian Doctrine. Vocation Clubs — Serra International for adults interested in fostering vocations to the priesthood, and Parish Groups with the purpose of interesting young persons in the priesthood and religious life — were promoted throughout the Diocese. The Cana Movement, in parishes, and the Family Life Commission, for the Diocese, dealt with Catholic marriages and family life issues. The Thomas More Society for Catholic lawyers, the Catholic Physicians League, and the Catholic Nurses League were also quickly put in place. He also fostered a Diocesan Council of Catholic Women, whose purpose was coordinating the efforts and activities of the various women's organizations. And, finally, mindful of the media's role and power, Bp. Dearden fostered *Carta* (the Catholic Apostolate to Radio, Television, Advertising) the Legion of Decency and an Office for Decent Literature.

Bishop Dearden, a firm supporter of new facilities to serve Catholics moving to the suburbs, presides at the 1954 dedication of St. Columbkille's School in Imperial.

THE PITTSBURGH CATHOLIC

From its beginning in 1844 the *Pittsburgh Catholic* was owned and managed by laypersons. Bp. Dearden wanted his own diocesan newspaper. In 1954 he purchased the *Pittsburgh Catholic* and established the Pittsburgh Catholic Publishing Associates of which he, as bishop, was the president.

ARCHBISHOP OF DETROIT

On December 18, 1958, Pope John XXIII transferred Bp. Dearden from Pittsburgh to Detroit. After nine years as the bishop of Pittsburgh, John Dearden was installed as the Archbishop of Detroit, Michigan, on January 29, 1959.

CARDINAL

A participant in Vatican Council II, Abp. Dearden was named cardinal in 1969. From 1966–1971 he served as the first president of the National Conference of Catholic Bishops and the United States Catholic Conference. "It is not an exaggeration to call him the father or principal architect of the NCCB/USCC." Abp. John May of St. Louis called Dearden "the key figure in helping the church in this country to implement the reforms of the Second Vatican Council and in guiding the bishops' conferences to the role they currently play in the life of the church."[4]

John Dearden died in Detroit, on August 1, 1988. He had served 50 years as a priest, 40 as a bishop and almost 20 years as a cardinal.

Bishop John Wright

Eleven

John J. Wright
1959–1969
Eighth Bishop of Pittsburgh

The eighth bishop of Pittsburgh had achieved national and international prominence long before his appointment to the Diocese.

John Joseph Wright was born in the Dorchester section of Boston on July 18, 1909. While a student in elementary school and at the Boston Latin School, he cultivated serious and life-long interests in academic and cultural matters.

At Boston College where, according to the 1931 Yearbook, he was the "outstanding scholastic figure in the class" Wright achieved honors in academics and public speaking.[1] As chairman of the Boston College debating team, he led his peers to victory over Oxford University. While in college, Wright worked for the *Boston Post* and in the Boston Public Library. Upon graduation from college, his life ambition changed from journalism to the priesthood. He entered St. John Seminary, Brighton, in the fall of 1931; a year later was sent to the North American College, Rome, for studies at the Gregorian University.

After his ordination in Rome on December 8, 1935, Wright stayed on for graduate studies and was awarded a doctorate in theology in 1937. His doctoral dissertation, *National Patriotism In Papal Teachings*, had been suggested by Pope Pius XI who was seeking data on the subject.[2]

While writing his thesis, and when on vacation, Wright worked in parishes in Edinburg, Scotland; Southwark, England; and in the Dordogne region in France. The time spent in these areas made a lasting impression on him and gave him a deep love for those countries — especially France and Italy.

Returning to Boston in 1938, Father Wright taught at St. John Seminary. He soon became a part of Boston's religious academic and cultural life.

In 1943, Cardinal William H. O'Connell selected Wright as his personal secretary. O'Connell died on April 22, 1944, and Bishop Richard J. Cushing became the next archbishop of Boston. Cushing retained Wright as his personal secretary and had him named a monsignor.

AUXILIARY BISHOP OF BOSTON

Three years later, on June 30, 1947, Msgr. Wright was ordained bishop and appointed auxiliary to the archbishop of Boston. One of his first assignments was Episcopal Moderator of the National Retreat Movement — a duty he relished throughout his life.[3]

While Wright was auxiliary bishop of Boston, Fr. Leonard Feeney, S.J., was the director of the St. Benedict Center, a chaplaincy frequented by Harvard and Radcliffe students. The Jesuit priest-poet-essayist was well know and much loved. He and Wright were personal friends long before Wright became auxiliary bishop. In fact, at Wright's episcopal ordination, Fr. Feeney gave him a copy of the poetry of Gerard Manley Hopkins, S.J. as a gift.[4]

Fr. Feeney became "stuck on one idea," as Wright phrased it. Interpreting St. Cyprian's words: "Outside the church there is no salvation" in the most restrictive manner possible, Feeney denied salvation to all non-Roman Catholics. On August 8, 1949, Fr. Feeney's view was rejected by the Congregation for the Doctrine of the Faith. Later on in the same year he was dismissed from the Jesuits and then, in 1954, excommunicated.

In 1954 — four years after leaving Boston — Wright delivered, in Worcester, a most interesting lecture on Jean Lefebvre de Cheverus,

Bishop Wright baptizes a young boy in 1962 ceremony at Annunciation Church, North Side.

Boston's first bishop. The lecture was an almost exact description of Bp. Wright's intellectual life and pastoral style. In that lecture, spoken before the Unitarian Laymen's League, Wright described Cheverus as a man of letters, a gifted preacher, ecumenist, a tireless traveler in spreading the Gospel and fostering the good of his people. Wright's hearers recognized the resemblance and understood why the people of Boston started calling Bp. Wright a second Cheverus.[5]

169

FIRST BISHOP OF WORCESTER

In January 1950, Worcester, Massachusetts, became a diocese and John Wright was appointed its first bishop. The task of organizing the new diocese seemed both easy and a joy to the 41-year-old bishop. Within a year, the Diocese had plans for a Catholic hospital, a busy Catholic Charities office, diocesan newspaper and the Cenacle Retreat House.

During Bp. Wright's days in Worcester, 30 parishes and ten schools were constructed. The Diocese was alive with all manner of new organizations and projects: Guild of the Holy Spirit for teachers, the Archangel Guild for the police, Our Lady's Guild for utility workers, the St. Michael Guild for firefighters, St. Thomas More Society for lawyers, and the St. Lucy Guild for physicians.

Wright's ability as a spiritual leader and an intellectual brought him to prominence outside the confines of the Catholic Church. He formed a firm friendship with Joseph L. Lichten of the B'nai Brith Anti Defamation League. From their friendship there developed a series of lectures on "The Person and the Common Good." Years later, Lichten was appointed — upon Bp. Wright's recommendation — a Jewish observer to the Second Vatican Council.[6]

EIGHTH BISHOP OF PITTSBURGH

After nine years in Worcester, Wright was transferred — at the age of 50 — to the Diocese of Pittsburgh. On Wednesday, March 18, 1959, he was installed as the eight bishop of Pittsburgh. Cardinal Cushing presided and preached at the St. Paul Cathedral ceremony. On the following Sunday, March 22, Wright hosted a reception for anyone who wished to meet him. At Duquesne University's Rockwell Hall, more than 25,000 persons came during an eight hour period to greet the new bishop.[7]

As the Episcopal Moderator of the National Retreat Movement, Wright came to know, and was very devoted to, the Religious of the Cenacle. Less than a month after his arrival in Pittsburgh, he wrote the Superior General begging for a Cenacle in his diocese. The request could not be honored until 1965 when, to Wright's delight and the

U.S. Senator Patrick McNamara of Michigan receives 1963 diocesan labor award from Bishop Wright. Looking on are Msgr. Charles Owen Rice (center) and William Hart of the Allegheny County Labor Council.

great spiritual good of the Diocese, the Cenacle Sisters came to Pittsburgh and opened a retreat house in Oakland.

Bp. Wright was a pioneer in and a strong promotor of the layperson's role in the church. As bishop of Pittsburgh he immediately placed laypersons on the Diocesan School Board, established a commission on Human Relations and fostered (especially through parish councils) lay leadership. Long before the Second Vatican Council, Wright organized a Diocesan Pastoral Council composed principally of lay men and women. Diocesan officials were required to attend the Council's meetings, but only as auditors.[8]

Anticipating the ecumenical openness of Vatican Council II, Wright

171

Bishop Wright visits with Pope Paul VI on Ash Wednesday of 1969 in Rome.

promoted Project Equality — an interfaith group concerned about equal employment opportunities. The Diocesan Ecumenical Commission, established by Bp. Wright in 1964, promoted — together with the Pittsburgh Council of Churches — "The Person and The Common Good" lecture series that Wright and Lichten had organized some years before in Worcester. The Christian Associates of Southwest Pennsylvania was an outgrowth of the lecture series.[9]

VATICAN COUNCIL II

Soon after John XXIII announced Vatican Council II, Bp. Wright was named a member of the Theological Commission of the Preparatory Commission of the Council.

Years after the Council experience, Wright would state that the most lasting fruits of the Commission's work included the "seed-ideas" of the chapter on collegiality, the chapter on the laity and the chapter on the Blessed Virgin in the *Constitution on the Church*. He also valued the "seed-ideas" of the section on the person, Christian anthropology, and the dialogue with atheism, marriage, peace and war in the *Constitution on the Church in the Modern World*.[10]

Wright was chairman of the Council subcommission which drafted the chapter on the laity in the *Dogmatic Constitution on the Church* and a member of the mixed subcommittee responsible for the chapter on "Marriage and the Family." He also served as a member of the subcommittee on "The Signs of the Times" and "The Church of the Poor." Among Bp. Wright's most memorable interventions during the Council was his address on the question "of religious liberty and its exercise" and its relationship to the question of "the common good."

In his important book, *American Participation in the Second Vatican Council*, Msgr. Vincent Yzermans sums up Wright's participation in the Council: "Bishop John Wright presented to his colleagues from other nations an image of the American bishop they were not quite prepared to expect."[11]

When he returned from the Council to Pittsburgh — after one of the sessions or at the close of the Council itself — Wright made it his duty through his writings, sermons, radio talks and a series of public lectures delivered at Central Catholic High School to share his knowledge of and experiences at the Council. And he maintained that it would take 50 years to realize what Vatican Council II was all about.

NATIONAL AND LOCAL LEADERSHIP

Alongside his duties as bishop of Pittsburgh, Wright was very involved with many aspects of the Church in the United States. On the level of the National Conference of Catholic Bishops, he served in various capacities and was chairman of the drafting committee for the first two post counciliar collective pastoral letters of the American bishops: *The Church in Our Day* (1967) and *Human Life in Our Day* (1968). He was also elected by the American hierarchy as a delegate

Dr. Regis Ging of the Knights of Columbus presents Bishop Wright with a check for $40,000 which the Knights of Columbus raised in 1964 for St. Anthony School for Exceptional Children.

Bishop Wright joins his two auxiliary bishops, Bishop John McDowell and Bishop Vincent Leonard, for the 1969 diocesan Clergy Day.

to the first two Synods of Bishops (1967 and 1969).

Bp. Wright had a deep concern for the poor. He took an active role in an inter-faith committee for better housing within the Pittsburgh area. In the Diocese he established a Fund for Neighbors in Need which directed monies and support to self-help groups.

The plight of the single parent was a special concern of Bp. Wright. He supported, visited and did all that he could for the staff and guests at Roselia Hospital.

Bishop Wright, a champion of ecumenism, addresses the Lutheran Church in America 1964 convention at Pittsburgh's William Penn Hotel.

THE UNIVERSITY OF PITTSBURGH

As Bp. Bosco has noted so well, Wright

> introduced the Pittsburgh Oratory into the diocese. As a neighbor of the University of Pittsburgh, and loving academia as he did, John Wright was always interested in the university. He had a pastoral concern for the spiritual life and growth of the Catholic professors, students, and staff who frequented the university. So he entrusted his concern to the Fathers of the Oratory, the sons of St. Philip Neri and Cardinal John Henry Newman, with the hope that they would bring, as indeed they have brought, a new dimension to the Diocese of Pittsburgh. By his interest in the university and through the friendships he established with the chancellor, provost, and the administration of the University of Pittsburgh, he remedied what was certainly a defect. Relations between what was known as a *Presbyterian* University and the Roman Catholic Diocese of Pittsburgh were not always what they should have been, but John Wright . . . brought about through the Oratory and his own personal contacts the now-happy relationship between the University of Pittsburgh and the Roman Catholic Diocese of Pittsburgh.[12]

BISHOPS MCDOWELL AND LEONARD

Because of his extensive international, national and local responsibilities, Rome gave Bp. Wright the able assistance of two auxiliary bishops: Vincent M. Leonard (ordained on April 24, 1964) and John B. McDowell (ordained on September 8, 1966).

DIOCESAN SYNOD

On December 8, 1968 — in commemoration of the 125th anniversary of the Diocese — Wright convoked the Eighteenth Diocesan Synod. The synod's aim and purpose was to implement in the Diocese of Pittsburgh the decrees of the recently concluded Vatican Council. In his "Formal Call of the Synod" Wright put it this way:

Ambassador Henry Cabot Lodge meets in Rome with Cardinal Wright, Bishop Leonard and Father Wuerl.

> What is the purpose of this historic Synod? It is . . . to apply to our diocese the teachings and spirit of the Second Vatican Council; not the one without the other, nor either without reference to the other, but both together, literally in the case of the teaching, fully in the case of the spirit. It is to do for the diocese what the Council sought to do for the Church . . . .[13]

CARDINAL

Bp. Wright was named a cardinal on March 28, 1969. On April 23rd of the same year, he was appointed by Paul VI the prefect of the Congregation for the Clergy — the Vatican Office responsible for the pastoral life and discipline of the diocesan clergy, as well as catechetical instruction and the patrimony of the church.

During his ten years at the Vatican, the Congregation — under Wright's direction — issued the *Circular Letter on Priest Councils* (1969) mandating diocesan priest councils, the *General Catechetical Directory* (1971) which formed the basis for directories by various conferences of bishops throughout the world, and the *Circular Letter on Pastoral Councils* (1973) which was a landmark for practical lay involvement in the local church.

In 1971, Paul VI appointed Cardinal Wright one of three presidents of the Second General Assembly of the Synod of Bishops — which produced the documents on *The Ministerial Priesthood* and *Justice in the World*. Wright was appointed to two subsequent synods: Evangelization (1974) and Catechetics (1977).

He was also a member of other Vatican congregations including those for The Doctrine of the Faith, Bishops, Education, and Evangelization and he served as a member of the Council for the Public Affairs of the Church, the Commission for Revision of the Code of Canon Law, and the Commission for Vatican City.

During the last years of his life Card. Wright endured a long and debilitating illness. On August 10, 1979 — at the age of 70, after having taken part in the election of John Paul II and while still prefect of the Congregation for the Clergy — Card. John J. Wright died in his native Boston. He was buried with his parents in the family plot at Holyhood Cemetery, Brookline, Massachusetts.

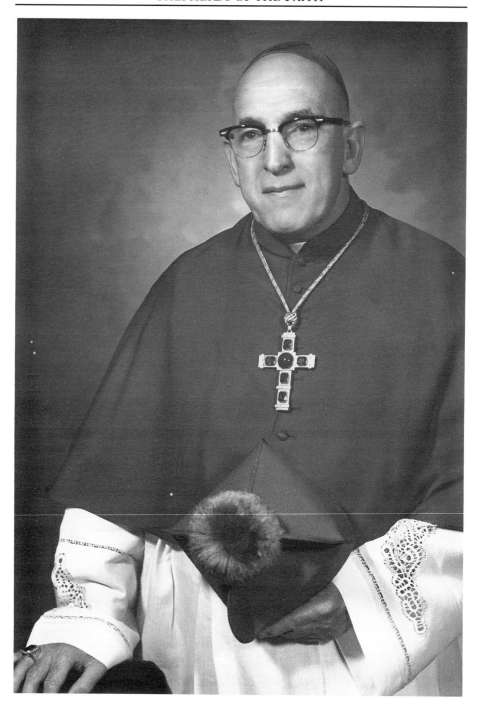

Bishop Vincent Leonard

Twelve

Vincent M. Leonard
1969–1983
Ninth Bishop of Pittsburgh

Vincent Martin Leonard was born on December 11, 1908 in his family's home, on Colwell Street, in Pittsburgh's Soho district.

He attended St. Brigid School and the Duquesne Preparatory School. It was during these early and formative years that Leonard, impressed by the Holy Ghost Fathers, decided to study for the priesthood. He entered Duquesne University in 1927 and was graduated in 1931.

In September of the same year, Leonard began his priestly studies and formation at St. Vincent Seminary, Latrobe, Pennsylvania. On June 16, 1935, Vincent Leonard was ordained a priest by Bishop Hugh C. Boyle, in St. Vincent Basilica.[1]

Father Leonard's first assignment was as an assistant to Father Edward J. Misklow, then chaplain at Mercy Hospital and chancellor of the Diocese.

In 1937, Leonard was appointed the first resident chaplain at the Allegheny County Home and Woodville State Hospital.

To better equip himself for this special ministry, Fr. Leonard returned to Duquesne University where he prepared for and was awarded a Master's Degree in psychology.

In 1950, Bp. Dearden appointed Fr. Leonard assistant chancellor of

Bishop Leonard moves in procession to St. Paul Cathedral for his 1964 ordination as auxiliary bishop.

the Diocese. The following year he was named chancellor. Then, in 1955, Leonard — now a monsignor — was assigned as administrator of Old St. Patrick Church in the Strip District. Four years after that, Msgr. Leonard became the vicar-general of the Diocese of Pittsburgh.

AUXILIARY BISHOP OF PITTSBURGH

On April 21, 1964 Leonard was ordained bishop and appointed as an auxiliary to Bp. John J. Wright; Archbishop Dearden delivered the homily at Leonard's episcopal ordination. From the St. Paul Cathedral pulpit, the former bishop of Pittsburgh said: "The priestly spirit and dedication of Bishop Leonard, his humility and understanding, his patience and his charity have endeared him to all who know him. Perhaps the finest tribute is reflected in the esteem and affection in

Bishop Leonard kicks off 1972 diocesan fundraising appeal with Auxiliary Bishop John McDowell and Matt Mahon, diocesan director of fundraising.

which he is held by the priests of Diocese with whom he has been so closely associated for so many years."[2]

For the next five years, Bp. Leonard — while continuing with his duties as chancellor, vicar-general, and pastor of St. Philip Church, Crafton — assisted Wright in the many facets of diocesan life.

NINTH BISHOP OF PITTSBURGH

In 1969 Wright was named a cardinal and transferred to the Vatican. On June 4, 1969, Bp. Leonard was appointed Wright's successor and became the ninth bishop of the Diocese.[3]

Bishop Leonard ordains young man to the priesthood in 1965 ceremony.

Bishop Leonard happily joins in the 1976 Thanksgiving celebration at the James P. Wall Home for the Aged, operated by the Little Sisters of the Poor on Pittsburgh's North Side.

Leonard was faced with a host of problems. With a population of approximately 900,000 Catholics, the Diocese of Pittsburgh was the second largest in the United States. The winds of change, prevalent throughout the church, were also blowing in the Diocese. Misunderstandings of the spirit and letter of the Second Vatican Council were causing confusion in liturgical practice. There was a serious decline in the number of priests and religious. Economic conditions in the Pittsburgh area were worsening as the steel industry rapidly declined and relocated from the area. And many of the social services and programs of the Diocese — up to that time central to Catholic life — were facing serious financial problems.

Bp. Leonard tried to address these and other problems. In his work

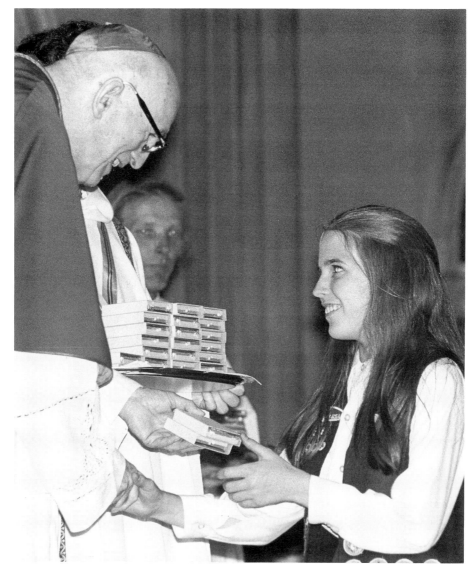

Bishop Leonard presents awards at a 1976 Scouting convocation.

and efforts he was assisted by two very able auxiliary bishops: John B. McDowell (ordained bishop while Wright governed the Diocese;) and Anthony G. Bosco (ordained on June 30, 1970).

DIOCESAN SYNOD AND LITURGY

The organization and implementation of the Eighteenth Diocesan Synod — convoked by Bp. Wright on December 8, 1968 — was one of the first tasks Leonard had to address. On March 25, 1971 — three years after Wright's announcement and two years after Leonard became diocesan bishop — the synod was opened at St. Paul Cathedral. It reviewed all facets of diocesan life, revised the diocesan School Board, proposed that women be considered for administrative offices at the diocesan, deanery and parish levels, gave greater responsibility to the role of dean and determined that assistant pastors would usually serve a five-year term, and pastors may retire at 70 but must retire at 75. The synod also established a Diocesan Pastoral Council, Catholic Charities Committee and a Catholic Youth Office. These decisions and others took effect on Pentecost, May 30, 1971.[4]

Bp. Leonard addressed the proper implementation of the second Vatican Council's directives on the liturgy by a pastoral letter directed especially to those pastors who were resistent to the changes.[5]

THE PARISH SHARE PROGRAM

During his first years in office, the diocesan financial situation was rather erratic, alternating between deficit and surplus. In an effort to bring about some stability, Bp. Leonard introduced a Parish Share Program. This program, started in 1979, taxes each parish on the basis of the parish's own income. The program brought greater financial stability to the Diocese and is still in effect.

CATHOLIC SCHOOLS

In 1970, John Cicco was appointed as superintendent of the diocesan schools. Cicco was the first layman to hold that office. Cicco, together with Bp. McDowell, the vicar of education, faced some serious challenges: the decline in enrollment and the necessity of closing some schools, a decreasing number of sisters and brothers in the school system and even a strike. In 1977, teachers in the diocesan high schools went on strike for recognition of a teachers' union and increase in salaries. The strike lasted for three weeks. It concluded when the teachers won their demands.

In order to promote and maintain justice and fairness for all members (especially the employees) of the Diocese, Bp. Leonard had, in July 1970, established the Due Process Board.

REORGANIZATION OF PARISHES

One of Leonard's saddest and most difficult duties involved the closing of churches as well as the termination of diocesan institutions and projects. But with change in population, decline in the birth rate, and deteriorating economic conditions, diocesan income decreased and decisions had to be made. During his years as bishop, Leonard had to merge three parishes (St. Bonifice, St. Cyprian and Mary Immaculate) into Our Lady Queen of Peace Parish; close and then reopen St. Boniface Church; and close the Bishops' Latin School.

RETIREMENT

On June 30, 1983 — in compliance with the new Code of Canon Law and the permission of John Paul II — Vincent M. Leonard retired as bishop of Pittsburgh. At his retirement, Leonard had been a priest for 48 years, a bishop for 19 years and the ninth bishop of Pittsburgh for 14 years.

Thirteen

Anthony J. Bevilacqua
1983–1987
Tenth Bishop of Pittsburgh

Anthony Joseph Bevilacqua was born in Brooklyn, New York, on June 17, 1923. He attended Public School 60, St. Thomas the Apostle School, and Richmond Hill High School. His deep admiration for a parish priest, Father Andrew Klarmann, determined a decision to prepare for the priesthood. He transferred to Cathedral High School, where he had a distinguished academic career. At the completion of his priestly formation and studies at Immaculate Conception Seminary in Huntington, New York, Bevilacqua was ordained a priest, in Brooklyn's St. James Cathedral, on June 11, 1949. His earliest assignments were as assistant at three parishes: Sacred Heart, St. Stephen and St. Mary Church, Long Island City. He also taught history, from 1950–1953, at Cathedral College.

In 1953, Bevilacqua was sent to Rome and the Gregorian University for studies in Canon Law. Three years later he was graduated — summa cum laude — from the same university. Upon his return to the United States, Fr. Bevilacqua served for one year as chaplain to the motherhouse of the Sisters of St. Joseph, Brentwood, N.Y. He served in the Tribunal of the Diocese of Brooklyn from 1957 until 1965, when he became vice-chancellor of the Diocese. During this time, he received a Master of Arts in Political Science from Columbia University and was a

Bishop Anthony Bevilacqua

professor of canon law at Immaculate Conception Seminary.

In the Diocese of Brooklyn, by 1971, more than half of its 1.5 million Catholics were immigrants. To serve this group and its special needs, Bishop Francis Mugavero established a Catholic Migration and Refugee Office and appointed Fr. Bevilacqua as director. In the same year he was appointed moderator of the Italian Board of Guardians of Brooklyn. Bevilacqua truly distinguished himself in these assignments. The volume of work for Brooklyn's immigrants necessitated the founding and organization of seven neighborhood offices in Brooklyn and Queens. These offices provided legal assistance, a Language Institute to care for eleven language groups, a program for refugees and a unit of the Apostleship of the Seas.

In addition to these duties, Fr. Bevilacqua was vice-chancellor of the Diocese and a student at St. John's University School of Law. In 1975, he was awarded a doctorate in Civil Law from the same university.

A year later, in 1976, Bevilacqua was admitted to the New York State Bar, appointed an adjunct professor of law at St. John's University and named a monsignor.

AUXILIARY BISHOP OF BROOKLYN

On November 24, 1980, Msgr. Bevilacqua was ordained bishop and assigned as an auxiliary to Bp. Mugavero.[1]

Together with his local duties, as an auxiliary bishop, vice chancellor, and director of the Migration and Refugee Office, Bevilacqua also served as chairman of two committees on the National Conference of Catholic Bishops: Migration and Refugee Services and Canonical Affairs.

His work on the Migration and Refugee Services Committee would oblige him to testify, in 1984, for a United States Congressional Committee concerning a Haitian Refugee Bill, and again in 1985 before a Senate Judiciary Committee concerning a proposed temporary suspension of the deportation of refugees from El Salvador. In 1986, Bevilacqua was again in Washington, this time to testify again about immigration reform.

The same work — together with his appointment to the Pontifical

Bishop Bevilacqua is congratulated following his 1984 admission to federal, state and county bar associations by attorneys Rosemary Corsetti, Nick Cafardi Jr., and Franklyn Conflenti (right).

Commission on Migration and Tourism — saw Bp. Bevilacqua journey to Haiti and Southeast Asia on fact-finding missions.

VATICAN ASSIGNMENTS

Bp. Bevilacqua's work on the Canonical Affairs committee associated him with a very delicate situation. In 1983, Agnes Mary Mansour, a Sister of Mercy, had agreed — with ecclesiastical permission — to serve as director of Social Services for the State of Michigan. When Sister Mansour declined to publicly oppose state funding for abortions, Abp. Edmund Szoka of Detroit withdrew permission for her to hold public office. Sr. Agnes Mary — supported by her religious community — appealed Szoka's decision.

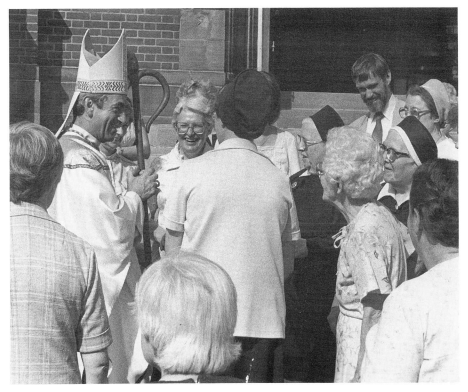

Bishop Bevilacqua visits St. Kieran Church, Lawrenceville, for 40th anniversary celebration of the diocesan ordination class of 1944.

The Vatican then appointed Bevilacqua to investigate the situation. The controversy — which ended with Sr. Mansour severing her ecclesiastical ties — received much attention and brought Bevilacqua both national and international prominence.[2]

TENTH BISHOP OF PITTSBURGH

Five months later, on October 18, 1983, Bevilacqua was appointed Pittsburgh's tenth bishop. He was installed as bishop of Pittsburgh in St. Paul Cathedral on December 12, 1983.[3]

Each bishop has, of course, his plan and method for the administration and direction of that portion of the church entrusted to his care.

Bishop Bevilacqua views 1984 St. Patrick's Day parade in Pittsburgh with Allegheny County Commission Chairman Thomas Foerster (left) and the late Pittsburgh Mayor Richard Caligiuri.

In March 1985, Bp. Bevilacqua set in place a new organizational structure for the administrative offices of the Diocese. A General Secretariat composed of four sections: Secretariats for Clergy and Pastoral Life, Education, Social Concerns, and Temporalities was organized to direct every aspect of diocesan life.[4]

And in December of the same year, Bevilacqua announced the formation of the Catholic Diocese of Pittsburgh Foundation. The foundation would establish endowments for the educational, social and administrative programs of the Diocese. Along the same lines, a Catholic Crusade for the Future was also part of Bp. Bevilacqua's plans; this aimed to obtain 30 million dollars over a period of five years.

A diocesan Finance Committee, headed by Auxiliary Bp. Bosco, was established in 1988. This 11-member committee — recommended in canon law — was to oversee diocesan temporalities.

Parishes, too were instructed by Bevilacqua, to form a consultative Finance Committee.

Bp. Bevilacqua did not limit ministry and pastoral concern to Catholics. In April 1985, when the employees of Wheeling-Pittsburgh Steel company were planning to resurrect the defunct steel operation, the bishop asked Pittsburgh banks to help. Together with other local religious leaders Bevilacqua also worked so that employees affected by closings would be guaranteed their pensions. And, in January 1988, the Diocese opened, for the unemployed, the Bishop Boyle Center — located in Homestead at the site of the former Bishop Boyle High School.

In Holy Week, 1986, Bp. Bevilacqua directed the priests of the Diocese of Pittsburgh to discontinue the practice of including women in the foot-washing ceremony on Holy Thursday. As a legal expert he concluded that participation of women was a violation of the rubric, or instruction, for that ceremony. The bishop explained his position: "I believe that the unity of the Church requires all Catholics to follow the teachings and laws of the Church. It is not possible for any individual, including myself, to ignore these laws for reasons of personal preference or convenience."[5]

Bishop Bevilacqua, explaining a bishop's symbols at Annunciation school on Pittsburgh's North Side, was a frequent visitor to Catholic schools in the diocese.

Cardinal Augustin Mayer of the Vatican Congregation for Divine Worship agreed with Bp. Bevilacqua that the liturgical rite in its Latin form indicates the washing of the feet of men. However, Bevilacqua appealed to the Committee on the Liturgy of the National Conference of Catholic Bishops. Their response was a memorandum that the variation from the exact words of the rubric was acceptable within the American Church. The bishop left the decision to the "prudent judgment of each priest in charge."[6]

SYNOD ON THE LAITY

Pope John Paul II appointed Bp. Bevilacqua to the 1987 Synod on the Laity. In preparation for the synod, Bevilacqua sent out a questionnaire to Catholics and clergy seeking input for his presentation. In Bp. Bevilacqua's address to the Synod — remembering the important role of his predecessor John Wright, considered by many the great theologian of the laity at Vatican Council II — Bevilacqua stated: "Twenty-four years ago this month, John Wright, my predecessor, as eighth bishop of Pittsburgh and later cardinal-prefect of the Congregation for the Clergy, stood before the fathers of Vatican II and pleaded for a positive statement on the dignity, vocation and mission of the laity in the church and in the world. Once this was done, he said, "the juridical bones of the church would come alive with theological flesh and blood."[7]

Upon his return to Pittsburgh, Bevilacqua noted that while there was a tremendous increase in all types of Church programs, little was being done to implement the proper role of the laity in the world.

BISHOP BOSCO

On April 14, 1987, Auxiliary Bp. Anthony Bosco was transferred to Greensburg. Bosco, a priest of the Pittsburgh Diocese for 35 years, was installed as the third bishop of Greensburg on June 27, 1987.

CARDINAL

Later that same year, on December 8, 1987, it was announced that Bp. Bevilacqua himself was to be transferred. After five years as the tenth bishop of Pittsburgh, Bevilacqua moved on to Philadelphia. He was installed as the spiritual leader of that archdiocese on February 11, 1988. On May 29, 1991, Archbishop Anthony Bevilacqua was named cardinal.[8]

Bishop Donald Wuerl

Fourteen

Donald W. Wuerl
1988–
Eleventh Bishop of Pittsburgh

Donald William Wuerl was born on November 12, 1940. He attended St. Mary of the Mount parish and school. There he met Father Joseph Bryan who inspired him to prepare for the priesthood.

After completing high school at St. Mary of the Mount, Donald Wuerl attended the Athenaeum of Ohio. He obtained a Basselin scholarship and earned a Master of Arts degree from the Catholic University of America at Washington, D.C.

Wuerl studied theology at North American College in Rome, and was ordained a priest in St. Peter Basilica by Bishop Francis Reh, the rector of the North American College, on December 17, 1966. He continued his studies at Gregorian University and obtained a Licentiate in theology in 1967.

SECRETARY TO CARDINAL WRIGHT

Returning to Pittsburgh, Fr. Wuerl was appointed assistant pastor at St. Rosalia parish, Greenfield, and part-time secretary to Bp. John Wright. At the same time he was a lecturer at Duquesne University and in the diocesan adult theology program. He also served as chaplain to the University Catholic Club.

Bishop Wuerl, then a young priest, joins his parents and Bishop Wright in celebrating on the day the latter was created a cardinal.

In 1969, when Bp. Wright was elevated to the College of Cardinals and appointed prefect of the Sacred Congregation for the Clergy in Rome, he requested that Wuerl serve as his secretary. This continued a relationship which had begun during the Second Vatican Council when the future cardinal often called upon the future priest to run errands and deliver messages.

For a ten-year period (1968–1979) Fr. Wuerl served as secretary to Cardinal Wright. He obtained a Doctorate in theology from the Angelicum — the Pontifical University of St. Thomas in 1974. For the next five years he was on the faculty of the Angelicum.

During the years that he was Wright's secretary, Wuerl traveled throughout the world with him visiting priests, seminaries and parishes. When in Poland, they were guests of Wright's friend, the Cardinal Karol Wojtyla.

In 1978, severe arthritis confined Cardinal Wright to a wheelchair and he required full-time assistance. As an aide to Cardinal Wright,

Wuerl was the only non-cardinal allowed into the 1978 conclave which elected Cardinal Wojtyla as Pope John Paul II.

Immediately after Wojtyla's election, while Fr. Wuerl was taking a shortcut through the Vatican corridors, he unexpectedly met the new pope. Wuerl respectfully and nervously dropped to his knees. John Paul II, ignoring protocol, asked: "What are you doing down there?" and offered his hand to the young priest. Their personal relationship was not altered by his election.

After Wright's death in 1979, John Paul II sent for Fr. Wuerl and remarked: "I understand you don't want to stay here any longer." Wuerl replied that he wanted to return to Pittsburgh and "do something more pastoral." Whimsically, John Paul II commented: "Oh, and what I'm doing isn't pastoral?"

RECTOR OF ST. PAUL SEMINARY

Once back in Pittsburgh, Fr. Wuerl served for one year as vice-rector of St. Paul Seminary. The next five years, 1981–1985, he was its rector. As rector, Wuerl reorganized the seminary program and encouraged the students to be more responsible for their studies and personal growth. He was a superb teacher who clarified difficult doctrines and theses. The students admired and respected him as he did them.

During his term as rector, Fr. Wuerl also lectured at Duquesne University, directed the diocese's Institute of Continuing Education of Priests, served as State Chaplain of the Knights of Columbus, and was a member of the Alumni Board of Governors of the Catholic University of America. He also was the executive secretary to Bp. John Marshall, the papal representative for the study of United States seminaries, and a consultor to the Sacred Congregation for the Clergy.

AUXILIARY BISHOP OF SEATTLE

On December 3, 1985 Fr. Wuerl was named titular bishop of Rosemarkie and assigned to be the auxiliary bishop of Seattle. Wuerl was ordained by John Paul II, in St. Peter's Basilica on January 6, 1986.

For the young bishop, the Seattle appointment was to be a difficult

Bishop Wuerl is ordained a bishop by Pope John Paul II in Rome in January 1986.

Bishop Wuerl's keen interest in Catholic elementary education is borne out in the dramatic increase in diocesan grants to those schools in the early 1990s.

challenge. Some time prior to his appointment, the Holy See had conducted an apostolic visitation of the archdiocese and had concluded that Archbishop Hunthausen could use the assistance of an auxiliary bishop who would take responsibility in specific areas of pastoral concern in the archdiocese.

This arrangement met with some opposition within the archdiocese and became a focus of national attention and considerable media concern. During this time, Bp. Wuerl carried out his pastoral ministry in the northwest while the Vatican assessed the situation.

In May of 1987, the pope appointed Bp. Thomas J. Murphy of Great Falls-Billings, Montana as coadjutor archbishop of Seattle and Wuerl returned to Pittsburgh.

ELEVENTH BISHOP OF PITTSBURGH

Nine months later on February 11, 1988, Wuerl was appointed and canonically installed as the eleventh bishop of Pittsburgh. He was liturgically installed in St. Paul Cathedral, on March 25, 1988.

The Diocese and the greater Pittsburgh community warmly welcomed him not simply because he was a hometown boy but especially because of his many pastoral, educational and administrative skills demonstrated through years of service to the Church.

DIOCESAN FINANCES

Although Bp. Wuerl would soon become known as a teaching bishop, his administrative abilities were challenged first. The Diocese of Pittsburgh had already exhausted all diocesan free reserves and was facing a $3.8 million deficit. Having identified his ministry as a new beginning in which "whatever we do, we do together," Wuerl appointed a special task force which made recommendations that reduced the deficit by $1.2 million and suggested ways to increase income.

Special incentive programs were developed to assist parishes with severe debts. A portion of those debts, totalling $1.1 million, were forgiven. Those parishes with large savings were asked to assist the Diocese. Over a three-year period, that ended in December 1991, almost $4 million was raised from investing the $14.6 million borrowed from 40 parishes.

The endowment drive to raise $30 million for the Catholic Diocese of Pittsburgh Foundation which had been inactive was renewed. And, after visiting the mission in Chimbote, Peru which the Diocese has helped to support for more than 25 years, Bp. Wuerl founded the Chimbote Foundation to ensure its continued financial support.

The long-range effect of these and other programs is that the Diocese has been able to achieve a modest surplus each year for the past three years. In an effort to continue this success, a diocesan Development Committee was formed to establish policies for all diocesan fund-raising appeals and to coordinate those efforts so as to provide responsible stewardship of all diocesan resources.

Catholic Schools

In his first pastoral letter, *New Beginnings in a Long Walk Together*, issued on September 28, 1988, Wuerl presented his vision for the future of the church of Pittsburgh in carrying out the work of Christ. He noted that the dramatic decline in local population, between 1976 and 1986, resulted in a loss of almost 113,000 registered Catholics, and had affected local communities, families, parishes and schools.

During that same period there was also a significant reduction in the number of diocesan priests and religious. Such circumstances, Bp. Wuerl said, challenge the laity to take their rightful place in the church and to use their God-given gifts in her service. To assist the church in this effort, plans for the establishment of an Institute for Lay Ministries were announced.

In *New Beginnings*, Bp. Wuerl wrote:

> If we are going to build for the future, consolidate, redefine, reorganize and re-evaluate the gifts that are ours, we have to share information and ideas with each other. We have to share our aspirations, our needs, our hopes, our dreams, and our data. We have to talk with each other. The process is consultation. We will, together, through various consultation processes face our future and its challenges, and work toward solutions.[1]

In that spirit, the bishop initiated a diocesan-wide consultation on Catholic schools. The purpose was to discuss every aspect of education in response to serious budget problems and the declining Catholic population. As part of a continuing program to reorganize for excellence, some schools were closed and others were merged. One of the positive results was the establishment of Oakland Catholic High School for young women in 1989. Programs were developed to strengthen the image of Catholic schools and to increase enrollment. Many schools hired development directors to assist them in fund raising. A new school subsidy tuition policy is presently being developed that will change the way in which Catholic education has traditionally been funded.

More significant is the fact that every Catholic elementary school in the Diocese has been accredited by the Middle States Commission on Colleges and Schools. When this occurred in June 1990, it marked the

205

Bishop Wuerl, who served as rector at St. Paul Seminary, has a continuing interest in the spiritual and intellectual formation of the men studying for the priesthood.

Bishop Wuerl was installed as chief shepherd of the Diocese of Pittsburgh on March 25, 1988.

first time that a major diocese had all of its elementary schools accredited by such a group. This educational excellence was recognized by local Catholic, Protestant and Jewish businessmen who established the Extra Mile Education Foundation to assist in the financial support of diocesan inner-city schools. Through June 1993, the Foundation had already contributed almost $5 million to this effort.

ADVISORY COMMISSIONS

With the publication of *New Beginnings*, Bp. Wuerl established a Diocesan Pastoral Council "to reflect the widest possible diocesan involvement in the consultation and decision-making process."[2] And, in order to involve as many laypersons, priests and religious in the ongoing activity of the central administration of the diocese as possible, and to benefit from their expertise and talents, Wuerl established a variety of advisory commissions.

The Justice and Peace Commission, the Worship Commission, the Commission to Counter Pornography, the Theological Commission and the Ecumenical and Interfaith Commission assist him in this effort.

Bp. Wuerl's desire to establish a spirit of consultation and collaboration became an essential part of his ministry. He has always emphasized that the members of the Priest Council are his closest collaborators in the governance of the Diocese.

BISHOPS MCDOWELL, WINTER AND TOBIN

In addition to Bp. John B. McDowell, who had been appointed auxiliary bishop in 1966, Rome provided Wuerl with two additional auxiliary bishops to assist him. Bp. William J. Winter was ordained on February 13, 1989 and Bp. Thomas J. Tobin on December 27, 1992.

PARISH REORGANIZATION AND REVITALIZATION

New Beginnings revealed the need not only for a reorganization of the diocesan central administration, but also for parish reorganization and revitalization. The bishop wrote:

We will make some changes so that the love and faith that is our Catholic Church — the beginnings of God's kingdom with us — will be shared and grow and live. Just as you and I shared that love and faith in one set of circumstances, the next generation — with us — will benefit from all the new circumstances that are this diocese as it grows, reorganizes and moves into the future.[3]

Spiritual Renewal

Wuerl's ultimate goal of reorganization and the primary concern of his ministry of service has been the spiritual renewal of the entire diocese. As he wrote in *New Beginnings*:

> Conversion, the daily turning to God in humility, trust and love, is the foundation and goal of all our efforts . . . Conscious of the call to holiness that forms us as a people of God, we need first to turn our attention to the ongoing spiritual renewal to which the Second Vatican Council challenges us and of which our daily Eucharistic Liturgy speaks. The task is to renew our living faith commitment in keeping with the teaching of Christ's Church.[4]

Bp. Wuerl's second pastoral letter, *Renew the Face of the Earth*, was written in 1989. It focused on the need for diocesan spiritual renewal. In that pastoral letter Wuerl stressed:

> Structures, programs, finances and resources exist for the spiritual life of the faithful so that we can carry out our mission. The Church uses institutions and money to help foster, share, develop and enrich the spiritual life of the Church. Our first priority, personally and together, must always be our spiritual life . . . how close we are to the Lord. We must continually ask ourselves to what degree does the Church of Pittsburgh resemble the kingdom of God.[5]

To help accomplish this goal, all the diocesan priests gathered, in the fall of 1992, at the conference center in Oglebay, West Virginia, for a three-day workshop on personal and spiritual renewal. The aim was to foster their renewal, so that they could then lead the same process in the parishes entrusted to their care. A diocesan Spiritual Renewal Committee was also established to recommend and foster the use of various spiritual renewal programs in every parish of the Diocese.

Bishop Wuerl's television program, "The Teaching of Christ," is shown on a commercial station as well as cable systems throughout the Diocese.

DIOCESAN POLICY ON CLERGY SEXUAL ABUSE

Wuerl's sensitive pastoral leadership was challenged almost immediately after his installation when in 1988 two priests were accused and then convicted of sexual abuse. In the midst of unprecedented media attention, he emphasized that the Church must act as Church when such allegations are made, while assuring that justice and compassion are provided for everyone involved. He created an Advisory Committee on Healing to review diocesan policies and procedures and to make recommendations on how to improve them.

When the diocesan policy on clergy sexual abuse, written in 1988, was publicly released in March 1993, he wrote in an accompanying pastoral letter:

Healing is an essential part of the church's pastoral ministry — a ministry that reaches out to all in need. In a proven case of abuse, particular care is directed to the person injured. Every pastoral and counseling means available form part of our ministry also to the family involved. We also need to offer pastoral care to the parish or other faith community affected. To heal this type of pain takes time, faith, care, courage, forgiveness and a great deal of love.[6]

The pastoral response of the Diocese to the issue of sexual abuse became a national model and Bp. Wuerl was called upon to share his views on various aspects of this issue at many national meetings convened to discuss it. Many dioceses contacted the Pittsburgh Diocese in 1988 and asked for a copy of these policies and procedures even before they were made public in 1993.

MIRACLE IN AMBRIDGE?

That same pastoral sensitivity was needed when in 1989 witnesses reported that the eyes of the corpus on a crucifix in Holy Trinity Church, Ambridge, had closed during Good Friday services. This alleged apparition received widespread attention by local and national media. People came from all over the United States to see this crucifix. A diocesan committee appointed to review these claims determined that there was no conclusive evidence that a miracle had occurred.

VATICAN ASSIGNMENTS

In 1988 Wuerl delivered the final installment of a seven-year study of Roman Catholic seminaries in the United States to John Paul II. Wuerl was the executive secretary to Bishop John A. Marshall, then bishop of Burlington, Vermont and papal representative for this special committee. Since 1984 Wuerl has been a consultor to the Vatican Congregation for the Clergy.

In 1990 John Paul II appointed him to be a member of the World Synod of Bishops held in Rome that year. Its theme was "The Formation of Priests in Circumstances of the Present Day." In his intervention, Wuerl stressed that priestly formation is a lifelong process. He highlighted four points: the importance of the ongoing formation process, the ecclesial and personal aspects of the process, a model and comprehensive plan for formation, and a proposal to encourage ongoing priestly formation.

About the importance of ongoing formation, Wuerl said: "Christ calls us to a perfection that is not quickly reached (cf. Mt. 5:48), to an intense living of all his gifts, especially love, which "'binds everything together in perfect harmony'" (Col. 3:14). Ongoing priestly formation involves continued growth and development of the person as well as the constant conversion of mind and heart. "If we have the duty of helping others to be converted we have to do the same continually in our own lives."[7] It is an expression for the priest of the universal call to holiness, a response to the primal and essential call of God. The call, even in the midst of weakness, to seek perfection follows on the Lord's word: "You therefore must be perfect, as your heavenly Father is perfect" (Mt. 5:48).[8]

NATIONAL LEADERSHIP

Bp. Wuerl has also served as chairman of the National Conference of Catholic Bishops' Committee on Priestly Life and Ministry, and a member of various other committees of the NCCB, including the doctrine, priestly formation and laity committees. His participation on these committees helped to produce an NCCB program on priestly formation and a document on priest councils, *United in Service — Reflections on the Presbyteral Council*. He is a member of the boards of North American College, Pontifical College Josephinum, Westminster College and the Catholic University of America.

CATHOLIC CHARITIES

As a part of his effort to improve the administrative structures of the Diocese, Wuerl examined the relationships of the Diocese with various church-related and community-based organizations. Catholic Charities received the greatest amount of attention.

In his pastoral letter *New Beginnings*, Bp. Wuerl noted that

"Catholic Charities is the primary diocesan agency responsible for sponsoring, coordinating, integrating, and delivering charitable services to people throughout the six counties of our diocese who have special and particular social needs which cannot be taken care of at the parish level."[9] In keeping with this statement, he established a stronger and closer relationship between Catholic Charities and the Diocese through the Secretariat for Social Concerns whose mission is to apply the Gospel command of love to the social systems, structures and institutions of society.

ECUMENICAL AND COMMUNITY AFFAIRS

From the beginning of his appointment as bishop of Pittsburgh, Bp. Wuerl has been very active in ecumenical and community affairs. A close relationship with the Jewish community has always been fostered. These efforts have brought him many awards and honorary doctorates from Duquesne University, Washington and Jefferson College, La Roche College and St. Vincent College.

He serves on the Council of Christian Associates, a regional ecumenical agency that provides ecumenical programming in the nine southwestern counties of Pennsylvania. He has helped to found the Christian Leaders Fellowship, whose members meet monthly to pray and study the Scriptures together, and is a participant in the Religious Leadership Forum which brings church and community leaders together to study important issues of common interest. He also is a cochair of the Greater Pittsburgh Race Relations Forum.

TEACHER, PREACHER, WRITER

There is no role, however, that Bp. Wuerl enjoys more than that of teacher, which is in fact the primary responsibility of a bishop. He exercises this role in many ways. A pastoral letter written in 1992, *Love and Sexuality*, was directed to young people and those who work with them. In it the bishop emphasizes how important young people are to the Church and he challenges them to live as Jesus has taught us.

Wuerl wrote:

> I am firmly convinced that you are not only capable of understanding what is right but that you are also able to make responsible decisions. Both you and I know that it is not easy. There is no easy solution to live. There are no quick fixes for the challenge of moral human living. But you are worth the effort.
>
> You should not be classified simply as a health problem or a birth statistic. You are a person made in the image and likeness of God with a future ahead of you. You are capable of living a moral and responsible life. Do not sell yourself short.
>
> In the power of the Holy Spirit, and in the joy of faith, Jesus' followers learned to live as he taught, and then to teach what he commanded. Today the Church must continue to proclaim Christ's teaching about love, marriage and the family. We do this to keep faith with our Lord. The most precious gift we have to pass on to you is God's word and the wisdom of two thousand years of human and Christian experience, alive in the Holy Spirit. This way of life with all its challenge and proven value is what we want to share with you so that our lives and yours will grow into the fullness that Jesus promises.[10]

Appointed as a Distinguished Service Professor at Duquesne University in 1990, he teaches one class or gives a public address there each semester on some aspect of Catholic faith. He has lectured on such topics as the Sacrament of Reconciliation and fundamental Catholic theology, and offered reflections on the papal encyclical *Rerum Novarum* and one hundred years of Catholic social teaching.

Wuerl has published many books, contributed articles on theology, philosophy, history and current events to various American and European publications including the Vatican's *L'Osservatore Romano.* Wuerl's books include: *The Forty Martyrs* (1971), *The Church: Hope of the World* (1972), *Fathers of the Church* (1975), *The Catholic Priesthood Today* (1976), *The Teaching of Christ: A Catholic Catechism for Adults* (1976, revised in 1984 and 1991); *The Teaching of Christ: Study Guide* (1977), *The Teaching of Christ: Abridged* (1979), *A Visit to the Vatican* (1981), *A Catholic Catechism* (1986) and *The Church and Her Sacraments: Making Christ Visible* (1990).

The bishop has produced catechetical audio and videotapes for national distribution, and writes a regular column for *The Pittsburgh*

Bishop Wuerl is well known for his commitment to persons with disabilities throughout the Diocese, including those enrolled in St. Anthony School for Exceptional Children.

Catholic. The Teaching of Christ: A Catholic Catechism for Adults, which he co-authored in 1976, has been a bestseller. It is now in its third edition and has been translated into more than ten languages.

His television program *The Teaching of Christ* is based on this catechism of the same name. In its fifth year of production, it is broadcast on KDKA, a local commercial television station, cablecast in more than 70 local communities, delivered nationally on the Catholic Television Network of America and airs nationally on the Eternal Word Television Network. Wuerl feels very comfortable in a pulpit, classroom or in front of a television camera. He is always eager to find opportunities to explain the teaching of Christ.

Some of the church and community issues that Bp. Wuerl has addressed publicly in a leadership role include abortion, school wellness clinics, a pastoral response to persons with AIDS, non-consensual historic landmarking, gay rights legislation, ministry to the aging, homelessness, services for unemployed persons, natural family planning and ministry to handicapped persons. These issues have been addressed in talks, in the formation of diocesan positions, and in his column in *The Pittsburgh Catholic*.

PARISH REORGANIZATION AND REVITALIZATION

Of all the challenges that Bp. Wuerl has had to face, perhaps none has been greater than the parish reorganization and revitalization project which he began to address in 1988. It is believed that a program of this type and magnitude has never been undertaken by any other diocese in the United States. Tens of thousands of people have participated in it through parish and cluster task force meetings as well as a questionnaire distributed to 40,000 members of the Diocese, of which approximately 20,000 were returned.

This effort has a history of its own. It has been the number one priority in the Diocese as it carries out its mission of spreading the gospel and serving people throughout its six-county area into the next century. This task has been made all the more difficult because of a dramatic population decline and shift, a decrease in the number of priests and a lessening of resources.

Bishop Wuerl receives an honorary doctorate from Duquesne University President John E. Murray, Jr.

The stated goal of the parish reorganization and revitalization project is

> to recognize and revitalize the parishes of the Diocese of Pittsburgh structurally, programmatically and spiritually. By this effort, this local Church in its parishes as communities of faith, and as individuals, strives to proclaim, model and serve the Kingdom of God more faithfully. We seek to accomplish this as a responsible steward of the gifts, talents and resources with which God has blessed the people of southwestern Pennsylvania.[11]

Bp. Wuerl set up an Office for Parish Services to coordinate, direct and manage this project. An Executive Committee was also organized to study and analyze data and to make recommendations concerning the parishes to be reorganized. Many documents were written to guide this process, including core values, general principles, a glossary of terms, communications strategies, a canonical assessment, property disposition guidelines, financial guidelines and personnel guidelines. It was also the stated policy of the Diocese that existing parish ethnic customs and traditions would be preserved.

The project started with each parish conducting a self-assessment on five essential areas: community, worship, service, education and administration. This first phase, conducted between October 1989 and June 1990, included a random sample survey of parishioners and key leaders, the formation of a parish task force and parish town hall meetings.

A second phase, conducted between October 1990 and September 1991, was called "realistic envisioning and collaborative decision-making." This involved a self-assessment of the viability of each parish in order to determine whether or not a parish was in need of major reorganization because of its particular situation, or as part of the cluster in which one or more parishes needed reorganization.

The third phase began in September 1991 and is called "collaborative planning and implementation." Using all the data gathered and fully analyzed from the first two phases, the Executive Committee established parameters and recommendations for each cluster of parishes. After many interviews and meetings, each cluster of parishes attempted to reach concensus on those parameters and recommendations.

Bishop Wuerl delivers homily at initial Eucharistic Liturgy of newly-formed St. John of God Parish, McKees Rocks in June 1993.

The great majority of people recognized the need for parish reorganization, even though it can be a very painful process, and have accepted diocesan recommendations. The reorganization aspect of this project is expected to be completed in 1994. Revitalization will be an ongoing process.

Because of concerns raised by ethnic parishes, Bp. Wuerl established a Commission on Cultural Diversity and instructed it to "submit a written report to the Executive Committee with recommendations, both on the diocesan and parish levels, on how to create parish unity and community based on the foundation of faith while respecting differing cultural customs and traditions."[12]

Thy Kingdom Come!

Bp. Wuerl's motto on his coat of arms is "Thy Kingdom Come." In *Renew the Face of the Earth*, Wuerl reminds us that truth, justice, peace, understanding, kindness, patience, wisdom, holiness and love are signs of God's kingdom among us. And although that kingdom will arrive in its fullness when Jesus returns in glory, it is already visible in the church.

As the Diocese celebrates the sesquicentennial of its founding, it looks to the future with hope because of the many faith-filled people who founded this church, met the challenges of their day, and contributed to its growth through many forms of sacrificial love.

Bp. Wuerl writes in *Renew the Face of the Earth*: "Our look to the future includes a vision of ourselves personally and as a Church growing every day closer to Christ. We see ourselves living ever more attentively the challenge: 'You shall love the Lord your God with all your heart, and with all your soul, and with all your strength, and with all your mind; and your neighbor as yourself.'"[13]

Notes

Notes to Indroduction

1. Kenrick, *Diary and Visitation Record*, July 25, 1836, p. 6.
2. Purcell, *Catholic Pittsburgh's One Hundred Years*, p. 27.
3. Kenrick, *Diary and Visitation Record*, p. 6.
4. Kenrick, *Ibid.*, p. 10.
5. Lambing, *The Catholic Church in the Dioceses of Pittsburgh and Allegheny*, p. 50.
6. Lambing, *Ibid.*, p. 58.

Notes to Chapter One

1. Morison, *Admiral of the Ocean Sea*, p. 15.
2. Eberhardt, *Survey of American Church History*, p. 8.
3. Nevins, *Our American Catholic Heritage*, p. 58.
4. Nevins, *Ibid.*, p. 55.
5. Lathrope, *Old New England Churches*, p. 61.
6. Eberhardt, *Survey of American Church History*, p. 179.
7. Lathrope, *Old New England Churches*, p. 61.
8. Purcell, *Catholic Pittsburgh's One Hundred Years*, p. 5.
9. Lambing, *Foundation Stones of a Great Diocese*, p. 29.
10. Purcell, *Catholic Pittsburgh's One Hundred Years*, p. 4.
11. Costello, *Lake Shore Visitor Register*, Dec. 4, 1953, p. 13.
12. Lambing, *Foundation Stones of a Great Diocese*, p. 27.
13. Lambing, *Register of Fort Duquesne*, pp. 57, 71.
14. Kent, *The French Invasion of Western Pennsylvania*, p. 69.
15. Lambing, *Foundation Stones of a Great Diocese*, p. 32.
16. Lambing, *Ibid.*, p. 34.
17. Lorant, *Pittsburgh: The Story of a City*, p. 20.
18. Lorant, *Ibid.*, p. 30.
19. Lorant, *Ibid.*, p. 34.
20. Lambing, *Catholic Church in the Dioceses of Pittsburgh and Allegheny*, p. 37.
21. Lambing, *Ibid.*, p. 38.

Notes to Chapter Two

  1. Walch, *Catholicism in America*, p. 3.
  2. Eberhardt, *Survey of American Church History*, p. 15.
  3. Brophy, *The Story of Catholics in America*, p. 10.
  4. Roach, *The Bicentennial History of Catholics in America*, p. 12.
  5. Roach, *Ibid.*, p. 17.
  6. Eberhardt, *Survey of American Church History*, p. 40.

Notes to Chapter Three

  1. Purcell, *Catholic Pittsburgh's One Hundred Years*, p. 15.
  2. Lambing, *The Catholic Church in the Dioceses of Pittsburgh & Allegheny*, p. 36.
  3. Lambing, *Foundation Stones of a Great Diocese*, p. 71.
  4. Kline, *The Sportsman's Hall Parish*, p. 9.
  5. Kline, *Ibid.*, p. 16.
  6. Kline, *Ibid.*, p. 21.
  7. Kline, *Ibid.*, p. 17.
  8. Kittell, *Souvenir of Loretto Centenary*, p. 229.
  9. Kittell, *Ibid.*, p. 54.
10. Kittell, *Ibid.*, p. 42.
11. Kittell, *Ibid.*, p. 43.
12. Kittell, *Ibid.*, p. 51.
13. Kittell, *Ibid.*, p. 193.
14. Kline, *The Sportsman's Hall Parish*, p. 23.
15. Kline, *Ibid.*, p. 27.
16. Kline, *Ibid.*, p. 29.
17. Kline, *Ibid.*, p. 29.
18. Kline, *Ibid.*, p. 33.
19. Kline, *Ibid.*, p. 34.
20. Lambing, *Catholic Church in the Dioceses of Pittsburgh & Allegheny*, p. 413.
21. Kenrick, *Diary and Visitation Record*, p. 5.
22. Lorant, *Pittsburgh: The Story of a City*, p. 58.
23. Starrett, *Through One Hundred and Fifty Years*, p. 77.
24. Hammill, *The Expansion of the Catholic Church in Pennsylvania*, p. 51.
25. Starrett, *Through One Hundred and Fifty Years*, p. 77.
26. Lambing, *Foundation Stones of a Great Diocese*, p. 44.
27. Lambing, *Ibid.*, p. 90.

28. Hammill, *The Expansion of the Catholic Church in Pennsylvania*, p. 52.
29. Maynard, *Great Catholics in American History*, p. 101.
30. Lambing, *Foundation Stones of a Great Diocese*, p. 149.
31. Curley, *Bishop John N. Neumann, C.SS.R.*, p. 100.
32. Purcell, *Catholic Pittsburgh's One Hundred Years*, p. 124.
33. Curley, *Bishop John N. Neumann, C.SS.R.*, p. 100.
34. Lambing, *Catholic Church in the Diocese of Pittsburgh & Allegheny*, p. 151.
35. Curley, *Bishop John W. Neumann, C.SS.R.*, p. 400.
36. O'Connor, *Business and Letter Record*, p. 1.

Notes to Chapter Four

1. Szarnicki, *Michael O'Connor*, p. 19.
2. Szarnicki, *Ibid.*, p. 19.
3. Szarnicki, *Ibid.*, p. 27.
4. Szarnicki, *Ibid.*, p. 34.
5. Szarnicki, *Ibid.*, p. 39.
6. Lambing, *Foundation Stones of a Great Diocese*, p. 90.
7. Heyden-Stillinger, *Pittsburgh Diocesan Archives, #391.* September 25, 1843.
8. Szarnicki, *Michael O'Connor*, p. 81.
9. Szarnicki, *Ibid.*, p. 63.
10. Szarnicki, *Ibid.*, p. 21.
11. Szarnicki, *Ibid.*, p. 75.
12. Szarnicki, *Ibid.*, p. 78.
13. Oetgen, *An American Aboot, Boniface Wimmer, O.S.B.*, p. 48.
14. Oetgen, *Ibid.*, p. 41.
15. Szarnicki, *Michael O'Connor*, p. 87.
16. Yuhaus, *Compelled to Speak*, p. 43.
17. Yuhaus, *Ibid.*, p. 53.
18. Yuhaus, *Ibid.*, p. 70.
19. Long, *Anti-Catholicism in the 1980's*, p. iii.
20. Long, *Ibid.*, p. vii
21. Szarnicki, *Michael O'Connor*, p. 115.
22. Szarnicki, *Ibid.*, p. 114.
23. Purcell, *Catholic Pittsburgh's One Hundred Years*, p. 113.
24. Szarnicki, *Michael O'Connor*, p. 120.
25. Szarnicki, *Ibid.*, p. 75.
26. Szarnicki, *Ibid.*, p. 118.
27. Szarnicki, *Ibid.*, p. 125.

28. McAvoy, *The Catholic Minority in Early Pittsburgh*, p. 79.
29. Szarnicki, *Michael O'Connor*, p. 144.
30. Lambing, *The Catholic Church in the Dioceses of Pittsburgh & Allegheny*, p. 78.
31. Kenrick, *Kenrick-Frenaye Correspondence*, #357.
32. Szarnicki, *Michael O'Connor.*, p. 142.
33. Szarnicki, *Ibid.*, p. 52.
34. Szarnicki, *Ibid.*, p. 142.
35. Szarnicki, *Ibid.*, p. 164.
36. McAvoy, *The Catholic Minority in Early Pittsburgh*, p. 82.
37. Szarnicki, *Michael O'Connor*, p. 126.
38. Hogan, *Peter E.S.S.J. Josephites*, March 15, 1989, Josephite Archives, Baltimore.

Notes to Chapter Five

1. Murphy, *A Reevaluation of the Episcopacy of Michael Domenec*, p. 15.
2. Hammill, *The Expansion of the Catholic Church in Pennsylvania*, p. 61.
3. Lambing, *The Catholic Church in the Dioceses of Pittsburgh & Allegheny*, p. 85.
4. Thurston, *Allegheny County's Hundred Years*, p. 59.
5. Murphy, *Reevaluation of Episcopacy of Michael Domenec*, p. 69.
6. Murphy, *Ibid.*, p. 69.
7. Murphy, *Ibid.*, p. 89.
8. Purcell, *Catholic Pittsburgh's One Hundred Years*, p. 43.
9. Murphy, *Reevaluation of Episcopacy of Michael Domenec*, p. 96.
10. Murphy, *Ibid.*, p. 99.
11. Pittsburgh Diocesan Archives, #997.
12. Szarnicki, *Michael O'Connor*, p. 167.
13. Congressional Record, March, 1918.
14. Nevins, *Our American Catholic Heritage*, p. 176.
15. Fink, *The Church in United States History*, p. 125.
16. Roemer, *The Catholic Church in United States History*, p. 254.
17. Fink, *The Church in United States History*, p. 126.
18. Murphy, *Reevaluation of Episcopacy of Michael Domenec*, p. 228.
19. Schmandt, *Records of the American Historical Society*, Vol. 101, p. 2.
20. Miller, *Records of American Catholic Historical Society*, Vol. 84, p. 127.
21. Lambing, *The Catholic Church in the Dioceses of Pittsburgh & Allegheny*, p. 491.
22. Lambing, *Ibid.*, p. 482.

Notes to Chapter Six

1. Lambing, Letter to R. H. Clarke, Nov. 23, 1886. Notre Dame Archives, #127.
2. Murphy, *A Reevaluation of the Episcopacy of Michael Domenec*, p. 357.
3. Murphy, *Ibid.*, p. 223.
4. Murphy, *Ibid.*, p. 304.
5. Lambing, *The Catholic Church in the Dioceses of Pittsburgh & Allegheny*, p. 105.
6. Murphy, *A Reevaluation of the Episcopacy of Michael Domenec*, p. 326.
7. Tuigg, Letter to Fr. Richard Phelan, Pittsburgh Diocesan Archives, #899, #1203.
8. Lynch, Letter to Bp. Tuigg January 29, 1876. Pittsburgh Diocesan Archives, #1350.
9. Tuigg, Letter, May 25, 1878. Pittsburgh Diocesan Archives, #1715.
10. Kittell, *Pittsburgh Catholic*, March 16, 1944.
11. Nolan-Tuigg, Pittsburgh Diocesan Archives, #1801, 1808, 1809.
12. Canevin, *The Diocesan Orbit*, 1816, *p. 25.*
13. Lorant, *Pittsburgh: The Story f a City*, p. 173.
14. Canevin, *The Diocesan Orbit*, 1916, p. 25.
15. Purcell, *Catholic Pittsburgh's One Hundred Years*, p. 52.

Notes to Chapter Seven

1. Purcell, *Catholic Pittsburgh's One Hundred Years*, p. 66.
2. Purcell, *Ibid.*, p. 57.
3. Eberhardt, *A Survey of American Church History*, p. 116.
4. Comes, *St. Paul Cathedral Record*, 1903, p. 14.
5. Lorant, *Pittsburgh: The Story of a City*, p. 218.
6. McDowell, *Epiphany*, 1984. p. 3.
7. Purcell, *Catholic Pittsburgh's One Hundred Years*, p. 55.
8. Hammill, *Expansion of the Catholic Church in Pennsylvania*, p. 78.
9. Hammill, *Ibid.*, p. 68.
10. *Pittsburgh Catholic*, March 16, 1944, p. 32.
11. *Pittsburgh Catholic*, March 16, 1944, p. 32.

Notes to Chapter Eight

1. Hammill, *Expansion of the Catholic Church in Pennsylvania*, p. 70.
2. *Pittsburgh Catholic*, September 4, 1902.

3. *Pittsburgh Catholic,* September 4, 1902.
4. *Pittsburgh Dispatch,* August 25, 1902.
5. *Pittsburgh Gazette,* August 28, 1902.
6. *Pittsburgh Catholic,* September 4, 1902.
7. *Pittsburgh Post,* December 16, 1902.
8. *Pittsburgh Catholic,* April 1, 1937.
9. *Pittsburgh Catholic,* April 1, 1937.
10. Woods, Edward A. Woods — Rev. Thomas F. Coakley. April 4, 1927.
11. Purcell, *Catholic Pittsburgh's One Hundred Years,* p. 70.
12. Purcell, *Ibid.,* p. 160.
13. *Pittsburgh Dispatch,* October 25, 1906.
14. Purcell, *Catholic Pittsburgh's One Hundred Years,* p. 169.

Notes to Chapter Nine

1. Purcell, *Catholic Pittsburgh's One Hundred Years,* p. 75.
2. Hammill, *Expansion of the Catholic Church in Pennsylvania,* p. 70.
3. Purcell, *Catholic Pittsburgh's One Hundred Years,* p. 78.
4. Dunlea, *Pittsburgh Catholic,* June 23, 1921.
5. *Pittsburgh Catholic,* July 3, 1921, p. 1.
6. Purcell, *Catholic Pittsburgh's One Hundred Years,* p. 75.
7. Purcell, *Ibid.,* p. 80.
8. Purcell, *Ibid.,* p. 79.
9. Hammill, *The Expansion of the Catholic Church in Pennsylvania,* p. 79.
10. Annual School Report, 1931, p. 6.
11. Purcell, *Catholic Pittsburgh's One Hundred Years,* p. 84.
12. Purcell, *Ibid.,* p. 84.
13. *Pittsburgh Catholic,* March 16, 1944, p. 41.
14. Boyle, *Mother Seton's Sisters of Charity,* p. 225.
15. Emerson, *Among the Messcalero Apaches,* pp. 162, 194.
16. *Pittsburgh Catholic,* July 7, 1921.
17. Lorant, *Pittsburgh: A Story of a City,* July 23, 1931.
18. Lorant, *Ibid.,* pp. 341, 562.
19. *Pittsburgh Catholic,* March 16, 1944, p. 48.

Notes to Chapter Ten

1. *Pittsburgh Catholic,* January 1948.
2. Hammill, *Expansion of the Catholic Church in Pennsylvania,* p. 73

3. Hammill, *Ibid.*, p. 74.
4. Hammill, *Ibid.*, p. 74.

Notes to Chapter Eleven

1. Congressional Record, May 22, 1969, p. E4251.
2. *Pittsburgh Catholic*, March 19, 1959.
3. Congressional Record, May 22, 1969, p. E4251.
4. *L'Osservatore Romano*, August 24, 1981, p. 2.
5. Congressional Record, May 22, 1969, p. E4251.
6. *Pittsburgh Catholic*, March 19, 1959.
7. Congressional Record, May 22, 1969, p. E4251.
8. Congressional Record, May 22, 1969, p. E4251.
9. Congressional Record, May 22, 1969, p. E4251.
10. Wright, *Resonare Christum*, vol. 2, p. 543.
11. Yzermans, *American Participation in the Second Vatican Council.*
12. Wright, *Resonare Christum*, vol. 2, p. 19.
13. Wright, *Formal Call of Synod*, R.C. vol. 2, p. 26, Dec. 8, 1968.

Notes to Chapter Twelve

1. *Pittsburgh Post-Gazette*, February 27, 1982, p. 7.
2. *Pittsburgh Post-Gazette*, July 3, 1969, p. 3.
3. *Pittsburgh Catholic*, July 11, 1969, p. 1.
4. *Pittsburgh Catholic*, March 25, 1971.
5. Pastoral Letter, January 22, 1971.

Notes to Chapter Thirteen

1. Installation Booklet, Bishop Bevilacqua, December 12, 1983.
2. *Pittsburgh Press*, October 19, 1983.
3. *Pittsburgh Press*, October 19, 1983.
4. *Pittsburgh Catholic*, March 15, 1985.
5. *Pittsburgh Catholic*, March 21, 1986.
6. *Pittsburgh Catholic*, April 18, 1986, *Origins*, March 17, 1988.
7. *Pittsburgh Catholic*, October 30, 1987; *Origins*, Oct. 29, 1987, p. 362.
8. *Pittsburgh Catholic*, June 3, 1991.

Notes to Chapter Fourteen

1. *New Beginnings in a Long Walk Together,* Sept. 28, 1988. p. 4.
2. *Ibid.,* p. ?.
3. *Ibid.,* p. 19
4. *Ibid.,* p. 20
5. *Renew the Face of the Earth,* Sept. 20, 1989. p. 3
6. Policy on Clergy Sexual Misconduct, March, 1993, p. 2.
7. John Paul II, Holy Thursday Letter to Priests, April 12, 1979.
8. *Ibid.*
9. *New Beginnings,* p. 15.
10. *Love & Sexuality,* March 15, 1992, p. 4.
11. *Reorganization & Revitalization in the Diocese of Pittsburgh,* April 15, 1909.
12. "Cultural Diversity," *Pittsburgh Catholic,* Jan. 22, 1993.
13. *Renew the Face of the Earth,* p. 30.

Select Bibliography

Almagno, R.S.	(1980)	*Cardinal John J. Wright, The Bibliophile.* Pittsburgh, Bibliophile.
Barcio, R.G.	(1991)	*Cathedral in the Wilderness.* Erie.
Barton, G.	(1897)	*Angels of the Battlefield.* Philadelphia. Catholic Art.
Boyle, Sr. E.	(1946)	*Mother Seton's Sisters of Charity.* Washington. Catholic University.
Brophy, Don	(1978)	*The Story of Catholics in America.* New York. Paulist.
Comes, J. T.	(1903)	*St. Paul Cathedral Record.* Pittsburgh. Colonial Printing.
Curley, M. J.	(1952)	*Bishop John Neumann, C.S.S.R.* Washington. Catholic University.
Eberhardt, N. C.	(1964)	*A Survey of American Church History.* St. Louis, Herder.
Ellis, J. T.	(1983)	*Catholic Bishops. A Memoir.* Wilmington, DE. Glazier.
Emerson, D.	(1973)	*Among the Mescalero Apaches.* University of Arizona. Tucson.
Fink, F. A.	(1948)	*The Church in United States History.* Huntington, IN. OSV Press.
Hammill, Sr. M.	(1960)	*The Expansion of the Catholic Church in Western Pennsylvania.* Pittsburgh.
Healy, Sr. K.	(1973)	*Frances Warde, R.S.M.* New York. Seabury.
Helbron, P.	(1985)	*Catholic Baptisms in Western Pennsylvania, 1799–1828.* Baltimore.
Heyden, T.	(1869)	*Prince Demetrius de Gallitzin.* Baltimore.
Kelly, G. E.	(1938)	*Allegheny County, Sesqui-Centennial Review.* Pittsburgh.
Kenrick, F. P.	(1916)	*Diary and Visitation Record, 1830–1851.* Philadelphia.
Kent, D. H.	(1954)	*The French Invasion of Western Pennsylvania.* Harrisburg.
Kittell, F.	(1899)	*Souvenir of Loretto Centenary.* Cresson, PA.

Kline, O. U.　(1990)　*The Sportsman's Hall Parish.* Latrobe, PA.

Lambing, A. A.　(1880)　*The Catholic Church in the Diocese of Pittsburgh and Allegheny.* Wilkinsburg, PA.

Lambing, A. A.　(1885)　*Register of Fort Duquesne, 1754–1756.* Pittsburgh.

Lambing, A. A.　(1914)　*Foundation Stones of a Great Diocese: Brief Biographical Sketches, 1794–1860.* Pittsburgh.

Lathrope, E.　(1938)　*Old New England Churches.* Rutland, VT.

Liston, P. F.　(1989)　*The Plundering Time.* Washington, DC. Abbeyfeale Press.

Long, K. C.　(1987)　*Anti-Catholicism in the 1980's.* Milwaukee. Catholic League.

Lorant, S.　(1977)　*Pittsburgh: The Story of an American City.* Lenox, MA.

Maynard, T.　(1957)　*Great Catholics in American History.* New York. Doubleday.

Miller, S. J.　(1973)　*Records of the American Catholic Historical Society,* vol. 84.

Morison, S. E.　(1942)　*Admiral of the Ocean Sea.* Boston. Little-Brown.

Murphy. Sr. C.　(1974)　*A Reevaluation of the Episcopacy of Michael Domenec.* St. Louis, MO. St. Louis University.

McAvoy, T. T.　(1961)　*The Catholic Minority in Early Pittsburgh.* Philadelphia. American Catholic Historical Society.

McCullough, C. H. (1989)　*Pillar of Pittsburgh: The Mercy Hospital.* Pittsburgh.

Nevins, A. J.　(1972)　*Our American Catholic Heritage.* Huntington, IN, OSV Press.

O'Connor, M. J.　(1841)　*Business and Letter Record.* Pittsburgh.

Oetgen, J.　(1976)　*An American Abbot. Boniface Wimmer, O.S.B.,* Latrobe, PA.

Piquet, C. J.　(1974)　*The Birth and Growth of Catholicity in Beaver County.* Beaver, PA.

Popp, Sr. C.　(1939)　*Sisters of St. Francis, Diocese of Pittsburgh.* Millvale, PA.

Purcell, W. J.　(1943)　*Catholic Pittsburgh's One Hundred Years.* Chicago. Loyola University.

Reese, T. J.　(1992)　*A Flock of Shepherds. The National Conference of Catholic Bishops.* Kansas City, MO. Sheed & Ward.

Roach, M.　(1975)　*The Bicentennial History of Catholic America.* Hackensack, NJ.

Roemer, T.   (1950) *The Catholic Church in United States History.* St. Louis, Herder.

Schmandt, R. H.   (1990) *Records of the American Catholic Historical Society*, vol. 101.

Starrett, A. L.   (1937) *Through One Hundred and Fifty Years: The University of Pittsburgh*. Pittsburgh. University of Pittsburgh.

Szarnicki, H. A.   (1975) *Michael O'Connor.* Pittsburgh. Wolfson.

Thurston, G. H.   (1888) *Allegheny County's Hundred Years.* Pittsburgh.

Walch, T.   (1989) *Catholicism in America.* Malabar, FL. Krieger.

Ward, M.   (1958) *The French in Western Pennsylvania.* Philadelphia. Catholic Historical Society of Philadelphia.

Wickersham, J.   (1920) *Kenrick-Frenaye Correspondence.* Lancaster, PA.

Wright, J. J.   (1985) *Resonare Christum*, vol. 1. Boston and Worcester Years, 1939–1959. San Francisco, CA. Ignatius Press.

Wright, J. J.   (1988) *Resonare Christum*, vol. 2. Pittsburgh Years, 1959–1969. San Francisco, CA. Ignatius Press.

Wright, J. J.   (1969) *The Truth That Makes Man Free.* Rome, Italy.

Wuerl, D. W.   (1988) *New Beginnings in a Long Walk Together.* Pittsburgh.

Wuerl, D. W.   (1989) *Renew the Face of the Earth.* Pittsburgh.

Wuerl, D. W.   (1992) *Love & Sexuality.* Pittsburgh.

Yuhaus, C. J.   (1967) *Compelled to Speak.* Westminster, MD. Newman Press.

Yzermans, V.   (1967) *American Participation in the Second Vatican Council.* New York. Sheed & Ward.

Newspapers

Lake Shore Visitor Register   December 4, 1953.
Michigan Catholic   January 29, 1959.
Pittsburgh Catholic   1844–1993
Pittsburgh Dispatch   August 25, 1902.
Pittsburgh Gazette   August 28, 1902, July 3, 1969, February 27, 1982.
Pittsburgh Post   December 16, 1902.
Pittsburgh Press   April 27, 1992.